W9-AVO-735
LOSERS CLUB
LESSONS FROM THE LEAST LIKELY
HEROES OF THE BIBLE
JEFF KINLEY
invert
ZONDERVAN®
GRAND RAPIDS, MICHIGAN 49530
www.invertbooks.com
ZONDERVAN.COM/
AUTHORTRACKER

Losers Club: Lessons for the Least Likely Heroes of the Bible

Youth Specialties products, 300 South Pierce Street, El Cajon, CA 92020, are published by Zondervan, 5300 Patterson Avenue SE, Grand Rapids, MI 49530

Library of Congress Cataloging-in-Publication Data

Kinley, Jeff.
The losers club : lessons from the least likely heroes of the Bible / by Jeff Kinley.
p. cm.
ISBN-10: 0-310-26262-3 (pbk.)
ISBN-13: 978-0-310-26262-6 (pbk.)
1. Failure (Psychology)—Religious aspects—Christianity. 2. Bible—Biography. I. Title.

BT730.5.K56 2005
220.9'2—dc22

2005024229

Some of the anecdotal illustrations in this book are true to life and are included with the permission of the persons involved. All other illustrations are composites of real situations, and any resemblance to people living or dead is coincidental.

Web site addresses listed in this book were current at the time of publication. Please contact Youth Specialties via e-mail (YS@YouthSpecialties.com) to report URLs that are no longer operational and replacement URLs if available.

Creative Team: Doug Davidson, Shawn Odegaard, Laura Gross, Janie Wilkinson, Holly Sharp, Rule29, David Conn
Cover design by Burnkit
Printed in the United States of America

07 08 09 10 • 10 9 8 7 6 5

DEDICATION

This book is dedicated to Joel Owens,
my closest friend and a fellow loser.

ACKNOWLEDGEMENTS

Thanks to Jay Howver and the rest of the crew at Youth Specialties for recognizing the potential for this project. I owe a huge debt of gratitude to my wife, Beverly, for her savvy marketing genius and for helping me create the Losers Club concept. Thanks to my three sons who are always willing to give me insight from a teenager's perspective. I am also grateful to Doug Davidson for his creative expert analysis and "tune-up" of my original manuscript.

CONTENTS

INTRODUCTION

This is a book *about* losers *for* losers. Now, don't get me wrong. I'm not implying you're a loser. Wait. No, I take that back...I confess. I *am* implying that. I do mean to say you're a "loser." But before you get offended and shove this book back on the shelf or use it for firewood, give me a chance to explain.

Over the past two decades, I have become friends with a number of guys and girls who have experienced some real losing seasons in their lives. For some, their struggles came in the form of doubts—times when they wondered what in the world God in heaven was really up to (or if he was up to *anything*!) Others experienced some pretty huge failures—failures that are documented as a part of public record. And others were labeled "losers" because they were nobody to speak of—they never made millions, achieved fame, or marked a generation. They were just people. But they are all part of a very special group, like a fraternity or sorority. Only it's a fraternity of *faith*.

A "Losers Club."

Now, this particular club has no official meeting place. No headquarters. No annual dues to pay. No special handshake. No identifying crest or logo. It does have lots of members. Just living life day-by-day gets you into the club. To learn the stories of its charter members, you need look no further than your own Bible. There, on the pages of Scripture, are the men and women who first signed the club's imaginary membership book—signed with their own sins, doubts, failures, and faults. If you saw only certain scenes from their lives, you might conclude they were long-term losers. But look at the entire movie, and you'll watch a doubter eventually believe, a struggler eventually overcome, and an obscure "nobody" eventually find a place in history—and in His-story.

Sometimes it's difficult to understand some of those biblical characters or make sense of the way they acted…or why they didn't do the things they should have done. It's also difficult because they lived in another place and time, miles and millennia away. But that's exactly why I wrote this book—to bridge that gap for you. Together, we'll remove the halo from the heads of these saints, ensuring they're not too holy for us to emulate or too ancient to understand. We'll see that they were *real people*…just like us (James 5:17). Each of them struggled with sins, doubts, and failures. I've yet to meet a young person who hasn't stared these same foes in the face. And for that reason, you may discover you have quite a bit in common with these people.

Losers Club will help you do several important things. First, you'll be able to *identify* with Bible personalities (perhaps for the first time), particularly in the struggle to believe we all have at times. Second, you'll be *encouraged* by those who, though they sometimes failed, still managed to rise above difficult circumstances to survive and to succeed. Third, you'll be *inspired* by the lives, exploits, and examples of some lesser-known characters in God's Word.

This book wipes the dust off 12 Bible characters, allowing them to step out of the pages of Scripture and into the living room of your mind. *Losers Club* reveals not only the humanity of Bible characters but also the humanity of our own lives. It links our pilgrimage to theirs, reminding us that doubt and failure are a normal part of the maturing process.

Losers Club will invite you to "re-image" your perception of some familiar Bible personalities while also introducing you to other characters whose stories you may never have heard. In the process, you'll discover that the questions we ask of God today are the same questions asked by great men and women of the past. Is God good? Is he there? Does he care? Is his timing perfect? How do I overcome my failures and struggles? How can an ordinary person like me make a difference?

In this book, you'll discover that it's in the middle of your struggles that you truly find God. You'll learn that it's okay to be a loser. (In fact, you might even find yourself liking the nickname.) And you'll realize that only through "losing your life" can you really find it.

This is a book for anybody who has ever lost a game in life. To be a part of the Losers Club simply means you haven't always "gotten it right." It means you have a scar or two from past battles or failures. It means you still struggle from time to time like the rest of us. It means you're encouraged and motivated by the stories and lives of others who struggled to become the people

God wanted them to be. It means something inside you refuses to give up until you cross the finish line.

If that describes you, then welcome to the club! You're about to begin a whole new chapter in your walk with God.

A Fellow Loser,

Jeff Kinley
Little Rock, Arkansas

P.S. Hope you don't mind that I called you a loser. Forgive me?

SECTION

FAMOUS DOUBTERS:

IDENTIFYING WITH SCRIPTURE'S STRUGGLERS

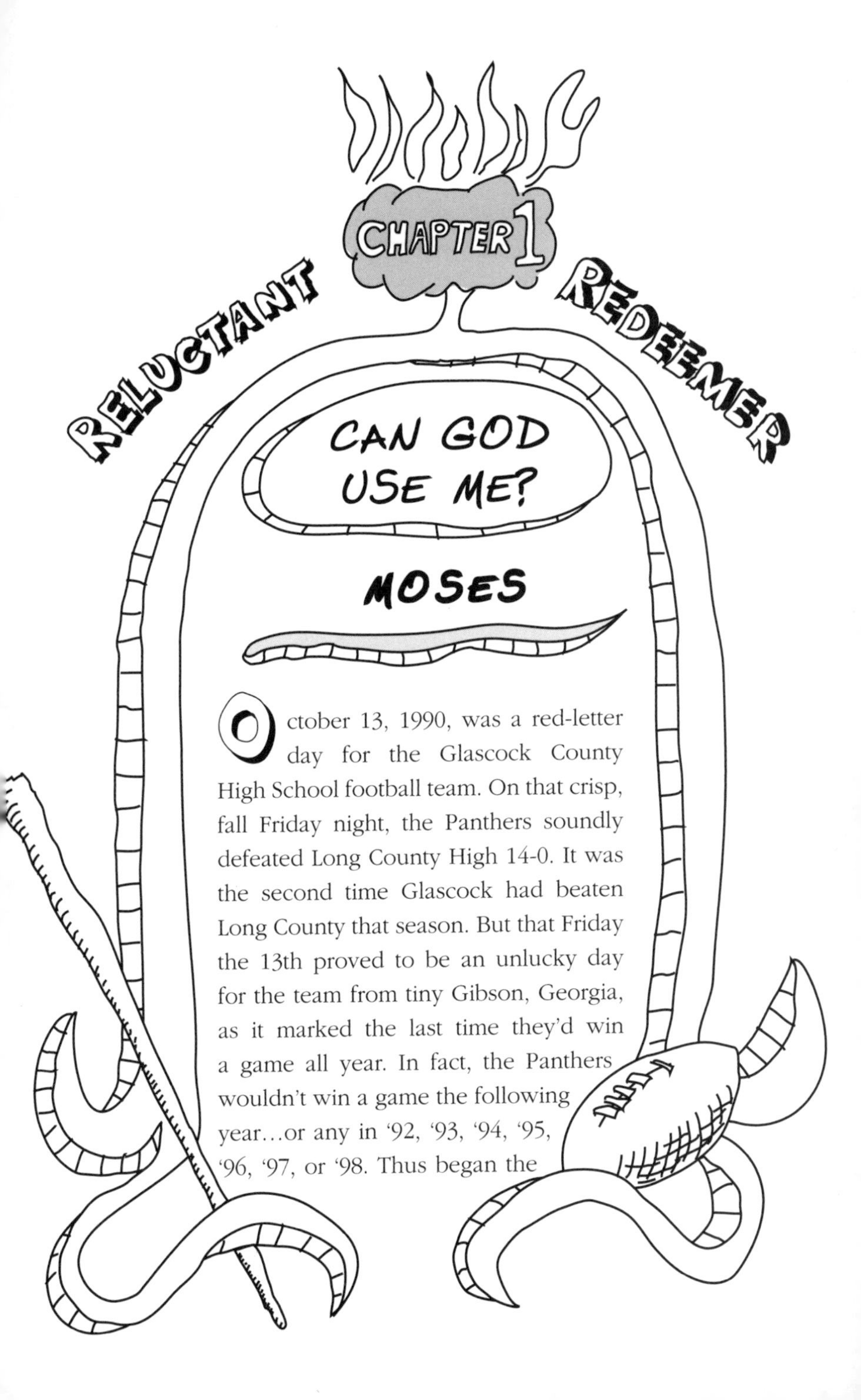

Chapter 1

Reluctant Redeemer

Can God Use Me?

Moses

October 13, 1990, was a red-letter day for the Glascock County High School football team. On that crisp, fall Friday night, the Panthers soundly defeated Long County High 14-0. It was the second time Glascock had beaten Long County that season. But that Friday the 13th proved to be an unlucky day for the team from tiny Gibson, Georgia, as it marked the last time they'd win a game all year. In fact, the Panthers wouldn't win a game the following year…or any in '92, '93, '94, '95, '96, '97, or '98. Thus began the longest losing streak in the history of Georgia high school football.

Season after season the Panthers struggled, only to lose game after game. With fewer than 100 boys in the entire high school, the "pickins," as they say, were slim. Nevertheless, each Friday night, all 15 players kept giving it all they had. Unfortunately, that wasn't enough. With most boys playing both offense and defense, there just wasn't enough energy in their adolescent bodies to outlast their opponents. They simply couldn't produce a win.

The streak swelled to 87 straight losses.

Now, imagine if through some miracle of time travel, Moses could step out of the Bible and walk into the Panther locker room after one of those heartbreaking losses. Moses might take a knee, look each one of those teenagers in the eyes, and say:

"Boys, I know exactly how you feel."

Now, you remember Moses. He's the guy who delivered Israel from Pharaoh, received the Ten Commandments, wrote the first five books in the Bible, and courageously led an entire nation for 40 years, ultimately taking them to the Promised Land. If that's the Moses you recall, then your memory serves you correctly.

But that was the "public Moses," the image his agent might sell to a prospective nation needing immediate redemption. That's the official portrait. You know, the 8 x 10 glossy.

There's another Moses. Same guy, just a different season of his life. We know his famous exploits, successes, and accomplishments, but what about his foul-ups, failures, and disappointments?

Is it really possible that Israel's redeemer could identify with a group of high school boys? Is it really possible that Moses could identify with us, in our own times of struggle, doubt, and failure? Did Moses ever have a losing streak? Let's take a closer look at this larger-than-life Bible character.

BACKGROUND CHECK

Moses was born during a difficult time in his nation's history, a time when more than a million Hebrew slaves lived in Egypt. With so many slaves living in his country, Egypt's ruler, Pharaoh (possibly Thutmoses I, or "King Tut" to us), became very nervous. Concerned about a possible slave revolution, he devised a sinister plan to kill all male newborn babies. (Nice guy, huh?). "Just throw 'em into the river," he declared. However, his master plan had one glitch. Jewish midwives assisting in the birthing process feared God more than any human leader, and they were protecting the newborn infants. It was the world's first Right to Life movement.

God blessed these women for honoring him in this way, and the Jewish population kept growing. One of those babies was born to a woman named Jochebed. After keeping her boy's birth a secret for three months, she could hide him no longer. So this mother made a difficult decision. She wove a "boat-basket," laid her baby inside, and placed the basket along the bank of the Nile River, hoping someone would find her son.

And someone did.

By "chance," while bathing in the river, Pharaoh's daughter found the basket. Feeling compassion for the child, she adopted him and began raising him as an Egyptian.

Little is known about Moses' next 40 years, but the Book of Acts tells us, "Moses was educated in all the wisdom of the Egyptians and he was powerful in speech and action" (Acts 7:22). In other words, Moses received the best education money could buy. An Egyptian education included studying hieroglyphics, mathematics, science, medicine, astrology, the doctrines of Egyptian religion, and interpretation of dreams. Moses probably spoke several languages and was destined for an influential government job in the mightiest nation on earth. He really was the "Prince of Egypt."

MID-LIFE MURDERER

However, later on something began stirring within this Hebrew hunk. Maybe it was a midlife crisis, but Moses wanted to know about his Jewish heritage and identity. Feeling a strong kinship with his people, he decided he'd rather live as a peasant Jew than as an heir to Egypt's treasures. Pharaoh must have thought Moses was crazy. How could he possibly do this, considering all Egypt had done for him? There was only one way.

By faith.

Moses took a huge gamble on God, choosing to go with his gut feeling instead of Pharaoh's fortune.

> *By faith Moses, when he had grown up, refused to be known as the son of Pharaoh's daughter. He chose to be mistreated along with the people of God rather than to enjoy the pleasures of sin for a short time. He regarded disgrace for the sake of Christ as of greater value than the treasures of Egypt, because he was looking ahead to his reward. (Hebrews 11:24-26)*

"Greater value than the treasures of Egypt?" Hello? Moses, do you realize what you're giving up? Think of all the good you could do for your people as an influential Egyptian politician. But you're throwing it all away for life as a slave! Where's the logic in that?

So Moses traded his cool, clean, comfortable bedroom in Pharaoh's fortress for the sweaty heat of a dirty mud hut. Lavish meals, servants, perks, popularity, and pleasure were all yesterday's news. Past tense. History. No more hobnobbing with heads of state. No more luxury, entertainment, or "easy street." The tenement tents of Hebrew-town would now replace his bird's-eye view of the pyramids. And to think, he traded it all away for a faint, faded promise that God made to Moses' forefather Abraham hundreds of years before.

> *"Through your offspring all nations on earth will be blessed."* (Genesis 22:18)

Moses had it all, but he gave it up because he believed God would bring salvation through the Jews some day.

Some might label him a loser for taking a gamble like that.

Later, Moses saw a fellow Hebrew being beaten by an Egyptian, and something snapped inside. Pouncing on the man like a desert scorpion, Moses murdered him in rage and then quickly buried the body in the sizzling sand. Unfortunately, news of the murder reached Pharaoh, and a posse was formed. If caught, Moses would surely face

a tortuous death...such as being buried alive with thousands of flesh-eating beetles. But let's not go there, okay?

Now with a price on his head, Moses fled to Midian, a few hundred miles away. Following his long journey, the 40-year-old fugitive quenched his thirst at a desert well (Exodus 2:15). Some women came to the well but were chased away by local shepherds. Moses defended the women and chased off the men. And to say thank you for this deed, Jethro, the father of these women, immediately gave his daughter Zipporah to Moses as his wife. (This gives the phrase "I kissed dating goodbye" a whole new twist!) Jethro also gave Moses a job watching sheep. It wouldn't be the last time a man went to work for his father-in-law.

So here's Moses, Pharaoh's former son, going from mega-wealth to mud huts to murder to menial labor. His dream of becoming a Jew again had taken an unexpected wrong turn.

Fast-forward 40 years. The sun is still beating down on the desert sand. The Jews are still suffering in Egypt, and Moses is still working for Jethro (not much room for promotion in the sheep-watching business). By this time, the power and promise of Egypt must have seemed like another life to Moses. Eighty years old, and what does he have to show for it? He's a senior citizen living in a tent in the wilderness. Hardly a success story, he's become the poster child for downward mobility. By now, he should be retired, buying ice cream cones for his grandchildren. Instead, he's on the back side of nowhere babysitting a bunch of stupid, stinky animals.

I'd say Moses was on a losing streak.

But sometimes God has to break us before he can use us, often using life's painful circumstances to do that. Maybe you know what I'm talking about. Maybe you've lost to someone inferior or you've been cut from the team, dumped by your girlfriend or boyfriend, or rejected or abandoned by a parent. Life sometimes involves losing. Some days you feel like it's just not worth the effort of crawling out of bed

So maybe you understand what it is to feel like a loser. It's during those experiences that you finally give up, lay down your pride, and surrender it all to God. At that point your brain fog fades away, your vision clears, and your heart reboots. It's time to hear from heaven again, and you're ready. You're finally humble.

That's where Moses is. He's had 40 years to think out there in the desert, and that isolation actually did him good, preparing him for a defining moment in his life.

BUSHWHACKED!

It was just another ordinary day for Moses. Wake up. Get dressed. Eat breakfast (a glass of goat's milk, scrambled eggs, NO bacon). Kiss the wife and kids, then trudge off to the sheep. And it's a shepherd's job to find green pasture for his sheep, so Moses led his flock to a grassy spot along the side of some mountain (a mountain he later climbed to receive the Ten Commandments). Perched atop a large rock, Moses was faithfully watching his sheep when something caught his attention.

> *There the angel of the Lord appeared to him in flames of fire from within a bush.*

Moses saw that though the bush was on fire it did not burn up. So Moses thought, "I will go over and see this strange sight—why the bush does not burn up." When the Lord saw that he had gone over to look, God called to him from within the bush, "Moses! Moses!" And Moses said, "Here I am." (Exodus 3:2-4)

Okay, picture this scene. There's a bush on fire. Not a big deal considering it gets hot in the desert. But this isn't a typical bushfire. This burning bush isn't burning up! Obviously, this phenomenon goes against the laws of nature; something very *un*natural is happening here.

Curious, Moses walked closer, and things got even more bizarre. The bush started speaking! A talking bush? This multimedia demonstration convinced Moses he was in the presence of the Almighty. This wasn't one of Pharaoh's fictitious deities. Oh no. We're talking GOD here…as in THE God of the Universe. Creator. Master. God of Abraham, Isaac, and Jacob. The real and true God.

This wasn't going to be an ordinary day after all.

God's voice called twice from the flaming bush. "Moses. Moses!" And as there were no sheep around named Moses, the shepherd man responded. Wouldn't you?!

"Here I am."

Moses was mesmerized. I mean, what an unlikely place to meet God! There wasn't a palace, temple, tabernacle, or church for hundreds of miles. No choir, music, or pipe organs. No pulpits, preachers, or pews. Just rock, mountain, and sand. A rugged wilderness sanctuary.

> *"Do not come any closer," God said. "Take off your sandals, for the place where you are standing is holy ground." Then he said, "I am the God of your father, the God of Abraham, the God of Isaac and the God of Jacob." At this, Moses hid his face, because he was afraid to look at God. (Exodus 3:5-6)*

Moses did exactly what anyone would do...he shook with fear. *God* was there! Traumatized by the presence of One who shakes mountains and commands thunder and lightning (2 Samuel 22:8-15), the shepherd hid his face, fully aware of his sinfulness. God's glory x-rayed Moses' heart, revealing every character flaw, moral defect, and human imperfection. And this drove Moses to his knees.

Right where God wanted him.

The Lord didn't come to *condemn* Moses that desert morning. Instead, he came to *call* him. Often we think of God as a celestial policeman who pulls us over only to write us a ticket. But more often, God asks for our help in accomplishing his will. And that was the case with Moses. God commissioned Moses with the task of delivering the Hebrews out of four hundred years of

slavery and oppression (Exodus 3:7-10). And while the exiled Jew must have enjoyed the divine attention, that little phrase "I am sending *you*" must have been a real shocker. Apparently so, for Moses gave God five reasons he was the world's most unqualified candidate for the job. In reality, they're excuses given by a man who believes he's a loser.

LOSER EXCUSE #1

"I'm a Nobody. Why Would They Listen to Me?"

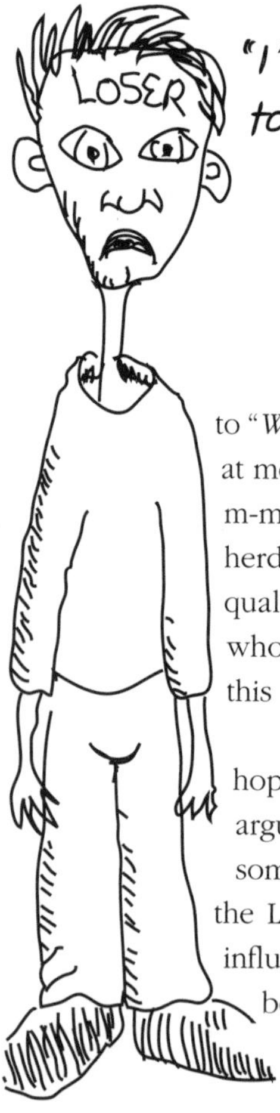

> *"Who am I, that I should go to Pharaoh and bring the Israelites out of Egypt?"* (Exodus 3:11)

Moses goes from "*Here* am I, Lord" in verse 4 to "*Who* am I, Lord?" in verse 11. "Come on, Lord, look at me!" he says. "I'm a fugitive from justice....a m-m-m-murderer for heaven's sake, an 80-year-old sheep-herder. For this mission, you need somebody who's qualified. Somebody with experience. Somebody who's...*somebody*. Not me. I'm the biggest *nobody* this side of the Nile!"

Moses began his protest by discrediting himself, hoping to convince God to rethink this bad idea. His argument is based on the belief that this job is for somebody "important." But while we might expect the Lord to use rich, intelligent, beautiful, talented, and influential people for his kingdom, that rarely seems to be the case. We think, *Wow, if Tiger Woods or Bill Gates were Christians, imagine what they could do for God!* But apparently God doesn't think that way. He delights in using ordinary people to accomplish his purposes (2 Corinthians 4:7; 1 Corinthians 1:26-29). This doesn't mean God never uses rich or powerful people. It just means he doesn't need human resources to achieve his purposes. He only needs willing hearts. When a common person accomplishes a God-sized task, only God gets the credit. And God likes it that way.

"It's not about who I call," says the Lord. "It's about who's doing the calling." Moses isn't being recruited for this mission so he can become a legend. The point is for Israel to remember *Yahweh's* name, not Moses'.

"The purpose in bringing Israel out of Egypt is so that they may worship me," God says (Exodus 4:23; 7:16; 8:1). And God wants Moses to know that he will be with him (3:12). Moses may be a "nobody," and you may be a nobody, too. But God is a "Somebody"! "*And that,*" he says, "*is enough.*"

Nice try, Moses. Score one for God.

LOSER EXCUSE #2
"But I Have No Authority!"

After his first attempt failed, Moses tried another approach. He asked God to excuse him from this huge task because he had no political clout, social influence, or respected voice in society.

> *Moses said to God, "Suppose I go to the Israelites and say to them, 'The God of your fathers has sent me to you,' and they ask me, 'What is his name?' Then what*

shall I tell them?" God said to Moses, "I am who I am. This is what you are to say to the Israelites: 'I AM has sent me to you.'" (Exodus 3:13-14)

God responded, saying influence and power aren't required for spiritual success. Popularity isn't necessary to influence others for God. Our confidence in serving God isn't found in our own reputation or resources, but in God. It's not about the messenger; it's about who sends the message. Think of the difference between a piece of junk mail and a letter from a friend. One you toss in the trash, and the other you can't wait to read. One you reject, and the other you tear into. And what makes the difference? It's the return address. A letter from a friend has immediate importance. The sender has value to you, so you read it with great interest.

Moses feels like a piece of junk mail. What he needs is a "return address," some way to convince Israel his message of deliverance is credible. In effect, God says to him, *"My name will be your return address, Moses. You just tell them 'I AM' sent you, and they'll believe you."*

Jethro's son-in-law needed absolute confidence his message would be received. Yahweh's personal name and authority would be that confidence.

God 2, Moses 0.

LOSER EXCUSE #3
"But I'm Not Persuasive!"

Okay, let's be real. Moses was no wimp. Forty years of intense heat, sandstorms, and other challenges of desert living had given him a thick skin and a tough mind. We see him applying that toughness as he tried to make his case against God's proposal. God answered each of Moses' objections word-for-word, argument-for-argument. But that didn't stop Moses. Next, he argued that even if he did go back to Egypt, he'll have no *proof* Yahweh sent him.

Good point, Moses. I mean, how would Israel know Moses was telling the truth? Anybody can claim to speak for God. How would Moses convince them he was their true deliverer and not just some guy with a huge ego? How would they know he was a prophet and not a lunatic? They'd have to see some ID. After all, it had been four hundred years since they'd heard from God. Moses had better have some proof he was who he claimed to be.

Moses figured this excuse was a safe bet. All he had was a *stick*, right? He could beat off a predator with his shepherd's staff, but imagine what two million people would say if he showed up bragging, "God has sent me to you people! And to prove it, look how cool my wand is. I can twirl it, toss it, and hit a wolf at 30 yards. I may walk softly, friends, but I carry a mighty BIG STICK!"

> *Then the Lord said to him, "What is that in your hand?" "A staff," he replied. The LORD said, "Throw it on the ground." Moses threw it on the ground*

and it became a snake, and he ran from it. Then the LORD said to him, "Reach out your hand and take it by the tail." So Moses reached out and took hold of the snake and it turned back into a staff in his hand. "This," said the Lord, "is so that they may believe that the Lord, the God of their fathers—the God of Abraham, the God of Isaac and the God of Jacob—has appeared to you." (Exodus 4:2-5)

Moses tossed down his shepherd's stick and it morphed into a snake, probably a cobra, causing Moses to run for his life! Duh! A *snake!* Wouldn't you run? But God's purpose here was to boost Moses' confidence. It was part of his ministry training. Moses picked up the snake, and it miraculously transformed back into his stick. God gave Moses miracle powers to convince everyone he was sent by God.

How odd. All Moses had was his pitiful stick, the well-worn staff that by this time had become like an old friend to him. God took this old friend and transformed it into a display of his power. Who would've thought?

Little becomes much when God is in it. Give a baseball bat to a ten-year-old boy, and he'll beat the backyard bushes into submission or persuade his little brother to do his chores for him. Give that same bat to a major-league slugger, and he'll rip a ball into the upper deck. It's not about the stick. It's about who's controlling the stick. It's not about the shepherd here. It's about the shepherd's Shepherd. If Moses was looking for persuasion, God's power would be all he'd need to convince his fellow Jews and future enemies he was the real deal.

God 3, Moses 0

LOSER EXCUSE #4
"I'm Not a Good Speaker!"

There's an illness in our land today, something that eventually infects most teenagers. In fact, it affects people of all ages. It strikes without warning. It can produce sweating, dizzy spells, nausea, vomiting, panic attacks, dread, trembling, stuttering, dry mouth, loss of appetite, and a host of other unreported side effects. For decades, it has been called the "greatest fear of Americans"—ranking above the fear of terrorism, death, and even acne! This illness sends paralyzing panic streaks down the spine.

What could it possibly be? A deadly virus, perhaps? Some new strain of Ebola? A form of inoperable cancer or communicable disease? Nope. Are you ready for this? Brace yourself. The number one fear of Americans is…

…public speaking.

Believe it or not, giving a speech before a group of people is enough to send most of us into an emotional tailspin. Maybe you've felt that fear.

The thought that he would have to deliver a speech before Pharaoh, the most intimidating man on earth, caused Moses to shiver in the desert heat. So he told God how he felt about it. (Apparently public speaking was the number one fear of shepherds from Midian, too!)

> *"O Lord, I have never been eloquent, neither in the past nor since you have spoken to your servant. I am slow of speech and tongue." (Exodus 4:10)*

Now let's be fair to Moses here. Most professional sheepherders don't have a lot of experience giving eloquent speeches. It's not likely that Moses enjoyed lots of long, enduring conversations with his lambs. So it seems a bit out of character that he should be a skilled orator. But remember, we've seen his résumé. We know he was educated in Egypt's finest schools. Make no mistake about it, this shepherd was nowhere near as dumb as his sheep. It was no accident that Moses attended the "University of Egypt." The Lord placed him there for a purpose, part of which was to get a top-notch education. And God could use that education and expertise—just as he uses your talents and gifts. God wastes nothing in your life. Same thing for Moses. Still, God reminds him: "Who gave man his mouth? Who makes him deaf or dumb? Who gives him sight or makes him blind? Is it not I, the Lord? Now go; I will help you speak and will teach you what to say" (Exodus 4:11-12).

"*Excuse me, Moses,*" God seems to say, "*but who invented humans and created the concept of speech? Who made the mouth with which you are questioning me now? You may think you're 'Slo-Mo,' but I'll help you, don't worry. I'll take care of you when you visit Pharaoh. In fact, I'll personally give you the words to say.*"

That's the same promise Jesus made to his disciples many years later (Mark 13:11).

Truth is, if God is on your side, no opponent can stand before you (Romans 8:31). It doesn't matter how "non-eloquent" you are. As long as you have God *with* you and his truth *in* you, you have all you need.

But even though Moses now has *four* strikes against him, he still isn't getting the point. Apparently his calloused feet have a heart to match, because he sets his stance in the batter's box and takes one more swing at God's burning fastball.

LOSER EXCUSE #5

"Just Get Somebody Else, Okay?"

Yahweh's logic and authority have annihilated every one of Moses' excuses. Down to his last bullet, Moses pulls out the only strategy left in his arsenal—the direct approach: "*But Moses said, 'O Lord, please send someone else to do it.' Then the Lord's anger burned against Moses*" (Exodus 4:13-14).

Oops.

God has officially had enough of Moses' pitiful excuses. God has clearly demonstrated his power and sufficiency in response to each excuse, so you'd think there'd be nothing left but for Moses to ask, "*Lord, where do I sign up?*" But it seems Moses left his pen back in the tent. His is a simple case of unwillingness and disobedience. You know it. Moses knew it. God knew it. Heck, even the sheep probably knew it! And this stubbornness is precisely what angered the Lord.

God conceded, allowing Moses' brother Aaron to speak for him, though Moses still wouldn't get out of all his speaking duties (Exodus 3:14-16). Bottom line: Moses would obey, one way or another. God wins again.

Shutout. No-hitter. Perfect game.

Now go back for a minute to that burning bush. If you were watching from beneath the cool shade of a nearby cliff, you might offer Moses some advice. After all, everybody knows you can see the game better from the sidelines, right? With that in mind, maybe you can agree with the following counsel.

Come on, Moses. Save yourself time and grief. Just obey God, okay? You know you can't outsmart him, so give it up, man. Enough is enough. Give in and get on with it.

Pretty sound advice, huh? But lest we set ourselves too far above Moses, let's place ourselves in his sandals, okay? Imagine a modern-day equivalent of Moses' fear factor. Instead of God calling you to barge into the Oval Office with a word from Yahweh, consider a scenario closer to home.

You're in *high school* and God calls you to run for junior class president. No big deal, right? Maybe. But realize you'll have to make speeches in front of the entire junior class. That alone might not scare the wits out of you, so let's add a little twist to your election campaign. Let's say God asks you to campaign on the platform of student-led prayer in school. And part of your strategy involves meeting personally with every student in your class to share this idea. Feeling a little hesitation now? Fired up about your mission yet?

Is it just me, or is it getting warm in here?

Placing ourselves in Moses' shoes does several things.

First, it gives us *understanding* of his hesitancy that day. We can sense the fear and emotions Moses experienced, how unqualified he felt. Imagine the huge question mark appearing in Moses' mind as he envisioned himself standing before Pharaoh. "*But Lord, I'm not a preacher.*" We can identify, can't we? *"Lord, you know better than I do that I am simply not 'class president material.'"*

Second, we are *encouraged* to know that Bible characters were people just like us. They weren't perfect; they were just like we are, with their own fears and weaknesses. And in spite of their shortcomings, God came through for them.

Third, it is *comforting* to know that whatever our need, God is *always* the answer. The mission may seem impossible, but we have a God who still works miracles. The greatest miracles are God's works *in* and *through* us.

So ask yourself, "*In the shepherd's shoes, how would I have responded?*" In light of this, can we cut Moses a little slack?

I thought so.

FROM LOSER TO LEADER

You know the rest of the story. Moses takes God's message to Pharaoh, demanding that Pharaoh set the Hebrews free. I don't have to tell you that his suggestion went over like a concrete balloon. Releasing the Hebrews would've brought Egyptian commerce to a screeching halt. Can you see the disbelief blanketing Pharaoh's face as he verbalized disgust for Moses and his God?

> *"Who is the Lord, that I should obey him and let Israel go? I do not know the Lord and I will not let Israel go…Moses and Aaron, why are you taking the people away from their labor? Get back to your work!" (Exodus 5:2,4)*

Eventually, God got Pharaoh's attention with 10 audio-visual lessons (popularly known as "The Ten Plagues"). Israel was freed and began the famous 40-year circular dance in the desert, journeying toward the Promised Land.

And Moses ended his losing streak.

"STICK" TO IT!

Moses doubted God's plan five times, and each time God answered his doubts while providing for his weaknesses. Moses learned his needs would be met through God's provision, not through his own power.

When Moses Needed:	God Provided:
Credibility	His Presence
Confidence	His Commission
Confirmation	His Evidence
Communication	His Words
Companionship	His Assistance

Moses' self-doubt was a clever disguise for doubting God's sufficiency. He focused inward, on *his* weaknesses. God wanted him to focus upward, on *him* and his resources. Times have changed since Moses' day, but the challenges haven't. And neither has human nature—with all our fears, doubts, inadequacies, and failures.

So what about you? What is your "mission"? In a sense, God calls us to a fresh mission every day. But whether you're called to change a nation or a neighbor, a country or a classmate, it boils down to trusting his resources, not yours. It doesn't matter *who* you are in this world. It only really matters *whose* you are. Maybe you've been on a losing streak recently. If so, take heart. Today could be your personal U-turn in the desert. Maybe this chapter is a sort of "burning bush" to you, helping you hear God's voice. If so, before you start making lame excuses as to why God can't use you, pause and take a long look...at *him*. Allow what you see to change your mind about your mission and about yourself. Then open your heart, grab your stick, and get after it!

By the way, in the fall of 1999, the Glascock County High School Panthers took the field once again, with most everyone expecting loss number 88. Instead, those determined boys played their hearts out and beat Cross Creek High 12-6.

The losing streak was officially over.

SLO-MO'S LIFE LESSONS

LESSON 1: When God calls you to a task, he always goes with you. **(Matthew 28:18-20)**

LESSON 2: You are God's chosen man/woman for your campus. **(Jeremiah 1:5)**

LESSON 3: Your godly lifestyle authenticates his message. **(Philippians 2:15-16)**

LESSON 4: Know God's truth and how to communicate it to others. **(John 17:17; Romans 10:17)**

LESSON 5: You may need the help of others in fulfilling your "God-mission." **(Hebrews 10:23-25)**

CHAPTER 2

WHEN GOD FEELS FAR AWAY

IS GOD REALLY THERE?

DAVID

Loneliness.

Few things in life are worse than that dark and empty place. You know the feeling—that season of the soul when you feel friendless, abandoned, deserted… *alone*. There's a quietness about this enemy that can drive you nuts. Your soul is still. *Too* still. And it's during that solitude that random questions camp out in your mind.

Why do I feel so alone?

Why doesn't God do something?

Father, don't you care about me anymore?

Lord, where are you when I really need you?

Hello? Are you even there?

And sometimes the only answer you get is stone-cold silence.

Edgy, bold questions. And yet they're honest thoughts from a heart that is holding back nothing from God. However, those long moments of solitude can eventually cause you to have some serious doubts about God. When God seems silent, aloof, detached, and far away, you may question the reliability of the Bible and prayer—maybe even the whole "Christian life thing."

Ever felt like that?

Chances are, if you've lived on the planet for very long, you have. And you may have wondered: *Is it wrong for me to feel this way? Am I weird or bad for having these thoughts?* Well, I don't believe you are. In fact, these thoughts are a common Christian experience. They happen to most every God-seeker. Just ask someone you respect, "Have you ever wondered if God was really there?"—and see what he or she says.

So don't condemn yourself for asking those questions. And don't feel "unspiritual" or conclude you need professional counseling. Quite the opposite—you should feel pretty normal. And that's a good thing.

Actually, there are lots of reasons you may feel God has moved away (or at least gone on an extended vacation!) For example, you might encounter loneliness

- When your parents don't understand you (grounding or exiling you to your room)
- When your boyfriend or girlfriend breaks up with you
- When you get cut from the team or squad
- When you sin or fail
- When your friends let you down
- When people reject or abandon you
- When you go away to college
- When God doesn't answer your prayers
- When God doesn't meet your expectations
- When you're hurting (or in trouble), and there's no end in sight

During those times heaven can seem a million miles away. The big question hovering inside your brain is: *What am I supposed to do?*

Good question. I mean, what does God expect of you when it seems like he's forsaken you? What's the *right* response? How can you know for sure he's really there? Is there anything you can do to regain your confidence and restore your faith?

To find the answers, let's visit a man who was perhaps the most authentic, honest person in the whole Bible. His name is David—but before you conjure up images of sheep, slingshots, and a sleazy rendezvous with bathing women, consider a more contemporary image of the giant-slayer.

Imagine a page in your school yearbook. Scattered on this page are photographs of a guy from the senior class (let's call him "Dave"). Pic #1: He's diving for a pass in the end zone. Pic #2: He's hamming it up in the lunchroom, riding piggyback. Pic #3: He's in front of biology class making a speech about evolution…wearing a gorilla suit! Pic #4: He's at a pep rally, this time dressed as a cheerleader, complete with a skirt, pom-poms, and pigtails!

That's Dave. Outgoing. Athletic. Musical. Friendly. Popular. Cool. An all-around great guy, right?

True, but underneath Dave's confident exterior is a 17-year-old who frequently struggles with loneliness. These feelings make Dave wonder at times if life is worth living. His dad travels a lot, and his mom resents it. So they argue and fight…a lot. Sometimes the yelling and screaming is directed at Dave. Some days the verbal abuse is so bad that he escapes to a nearby park, where he sits and thinks. In those moments, his girlfriend, friends, teammates, and even his popularity mean absolutely nothing to him. They are powerless to fill the loneliness he feels deep inside.

Dave is not a happy guy. And so he asks: *Why me? Why do my own parents hate me? Why do I feel so alone?*

CAVE MAN

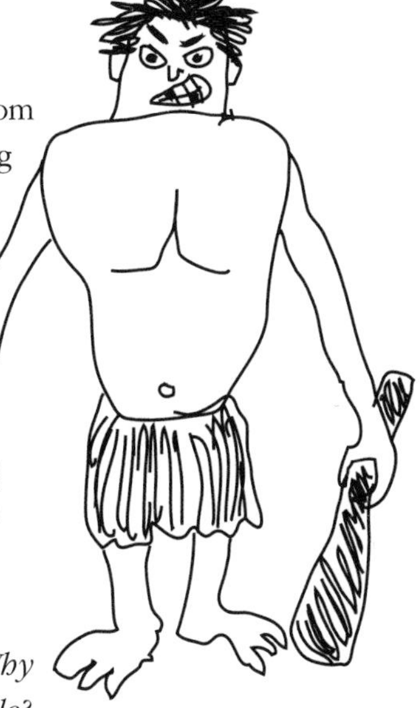

Okay, so that's not exactly the David from Scripture, but there are some amazing similarities. Like Dave, King David was musical, athletic, outgoing, talented, and popular. This David was also abused and rejected by people he admired. That caused him to retreat to a secluded spot (often a cave) where he composed his thoughts and dealt with his emotions. Check out a few of his recorded thoughts:

- *Why, O Lord, do you stand far off? Why do you hide yourself in times of trouble?* (Psalm 10:1)

-  *How long, O Lord? Will you forget me forever? How long will you hide your face from me? How long must I wrestle with my thoughts and every day have sorrow in my heart?* (Psalm 13:1-2)

- *My God, my God, why have you forsaken me? Why are you so far from saving me, so far from the words of my groaning? O my God, I cry out by day, but you do not answer, by night, and am not silent.* (Psalm 22:1-2)

- *My soul thirsts for God, for the living God. When can I go and meet with God? My tears have been my food day and night while men say to me all day long, "Where is your God?"...I say to God my Rock, "Why have you forgotten me?"* (Psalm 42:2-3, 9)

These are not the words of someone filled with the "joy of the Lord."

But they are the words of an honest person. David is saying: *God, where are you? Why is this happening? I don't get it. What did I do wrong? Are you punishing me? Why have you left me when I need you the most? People are watching, God. If you're really there, please show my enemies you're real! Do something... Anything to let me know you're still with me! Show me you still care. Give me a sign!*

Do any of those questions sound familiar? Ever felt this way? David did, and that's exactly what qualifies him as one of our "doubters." You may have wondered: *Are godly people supposed to feel this way? Is it okay to question God?*

The answer is yes. God doesn't ask that we never question him. Godliness doesn't mean we never have doubts. It isn't about *perfection*. It's about *process* — process and progress towards maturity. David was in the middle of this process. And so are you.

Think about David's gut-level honesty. He wasn't afraid to express his deepest thoughts to God. Of course, he probably didn't know the whole world would read them one day! Still, this refreshing honesty helps us identify with him. He was free to tell God anything he felt, a freedom you still have today (Philippians 4:6-7; 1 Peter 5:7).

Picture David in a mountain cave. It's midnight and raining. Warming himself beside a small fire, he wraps up in a blanket on his dirt mattress. Feeling like a castaway, David is befriended only by an occasional desert lizard scurrying by. He stares zombie-like into the flickering flame. King Saul, a man David

admires and longs to please, is trying to kill him. Unsure of what tomorrow may bring, David wonders where God is in all this. Sad in his solitary seclusion, he asks the same questions you ask in your loneliest moments. And when the response is a disturbing silence, a tremor reverberates through his faith.

HOOKED ON A FEELING

Can you understand why David felt like God had abandoned him? Remember, this is the same David who was used to spending hours alone in the wilderness caring for his sheep. This is the guy who courageously stood up against a giant and single-handedly killed bears, lions, and wild beasts (1 Samuel 17:34-37). This is the same David who wrote all those awesome worship songs, a man who had become a living legend to his people. He had often seen God's power deliver him from his enemies.

But now he was facing a brand new enemy, one more frightening than the jaws of a lion or the spear of a giant. Sure, those enemies could kill his body, but this one was tormenting his soul! And for David, that was something *worse* than death.

So there he was, cowering in a cave, wondering where to find God.

Of course, it's not as if he were denying God's *existence* or even questioning his *power* to deliver him. He wasn't questioning God's reality, just his *presence*. David knew God was out there. He just wasn't convinced that God was there with him. He wondered if God cared for him anymore.

David knew God was with him in battle with a visible enemy. That was easy. This wasn't so easy. The question was, *Would God be there with him when it really mattered?*

If we're honest, I think we've all wondered that. We've all spent time in the "Doubter's Section" of the Losers Club. People just like you (and some more mature than you) have known that same lonely feeling inside. They've had the haunting suspicion that God sneaked out of their lives in the middle of the night without leaving a forwarding address! I have had these doubts. So has your youth minister, your favorite Christian recording artist, your pastor, famous missionaries...even legends of the faith. Even people like David.

That's why you should have hope. In the loneliest days of your life—when so much is uncertain—you can be confident of one thing: You are not alone in your struggle.

You're not sinful or "backsliding." And God never intended for you to handle this crisis by yourself. No matter what painful circumstances you face, he wants to comfort you with this fact—others understand exactly what you're going through (1 Peter 5:9).

There's something else. Something even better than that. God also wants you to know that, no matter how alone you feel, he will never, ever leave you, not even in your most desperate, dark moments. No matter who else may have left you or let you down, God says he never will. That's a promise you can count on.

That may be true, you're thinking. *But during those times, I still* feel *like he's far from me*. I know. Many times I, too, have felt like heaven was outside my cell phone's calling area: "God, can you hear me now?...Can you hear me now?" But let me share a personal experience that might help.

A while back, I had root canal surgery. That's when the dentist takes this mini-jackhammer power drill, shoves it in your mouth, and starts excavating (sound fun?). Then he grabs this tiny razor-hook thing and carves his initials into your cheek (just kidding). Actually, he carves out the nerves in your tooth. In case you're wondering, this can be a very painful experience. That's why he first injects Novocaine into your gums. This drug numbs the side of your face, tricking your mind into thinking there's no pain in your mouth. Then "Dr. Drillmeister" can operate without causing pain.

Still, I wasn't taking any chances, so I requested nitrous oxide, better known as "laughing gas." Hey, if somebody's ramming a power tool in my mouth, I'm doing whatever it takes to avoid pain. (I hate pain!)

After a minute of breathing "laughing gas," I was feeling really good—so good I didn't care anymore what the dentist did to me. The gas diverted my thoughts about pain, allowing me to focus on more pleasant images, such as soaring through the sky like Superman and fighting six-headed aliens in the South American jungle. (Okay, I'm weird.)

Anyway, if you had asked me during that dental procedure if there was a hole in my tooth, I would have said "No." I felt no pain because of the Novocaine and nitrous oxide. Besides, I was far too busy battling alien predators in the Amazon! My point (and I do have one) is that while under the influence of the jaw-numbing drug, I was incapable of knowing the truth about what was *real*. I was only able to tell you what I *felt*. For me, feeling and reality were two different things that day.

That, my friend, is what happens when you go through life's lonely seasons. Your mind and heart are bombarded with so many thoughts and feelings it's hard to tell the difference between reality and illusion. When you feel as though God is far away, you need to recognize that your feelings don't always tell you the truth. Feelings easily manipulate, often misleading you. During those lonely times your emotions can "numb" you to God's presence, lying to you about what is real.

That's why they can't be trusted.

Bad days will come—sometimes like a sudden tornado, and sometimes like a slow train. Either way, you may end up in a lonely place, feeling devastated, abandoned, and orphaned. You may feel like your faith is in a nose-dive. What you need in those moments is something to hang on to, a lifeline connecting you to something solid and unchanging. That lifeline is a promise, a promise personally and permanently made to you by God himself. Here it is:

> *Never will I leave you; never will I forsake you (Hebrews 13:5).*

Simple, huh? Yes. But easy to believe? Not always. Again, that's why you have to recognize that your feelings may not be based on fact.

But wait a minute, you're saying. *The book of Hebrews wasn't written yet. So David didn't actually have that promise, right?* Well, no and yes. The writer of Hebrews is actually quoting Deuteronomy 31:6 (one of only five Bible books written by David's time). Because he knew Scripture, David knew God originally spoke those words to his people during a lonely and fearful time. About to enter the Promised Land after wandering the desert for 40 years, the people were terrified of the barbarian armies waiting for them there. So God gave them this promise, reassuring them of his presence. No matter how big their enemies, no matter how afraid or alone they felt, they could be certain God would always be with them every step of the way.

It's possible that David reflected on this truth while in that cave. In the silence of his soul, David reached a critical crossroads. He could choose to believe what his circumstances and emotions were screaming inside—that God had left him and he was all alone. Or he could choose to believe God's Word—that no matter how bad things got, Yahweh would be near him. It all boiled down to a personal choice.

BELIEVING IS SEEING

Maybe you don't spend much time hiding in caves. But you may sit alone in your bedroom (perhaps nicknamed "the cave" by your mom). Or you just may occasionally come to a place in life where God seems far away. In those moments, you too have a critical choice to make, one nobody else can make for you. This one is *your* call. It's a choice between believing what you might feel and believing what you read in his Word. It's a choice between depending on your emotions and depending on God's promise. It's your voice versus his.

It's a decision of *faith*.

Admittedly, it's not often an easy decision. We're all human, used to trusting what we can taste, touch, see, hear, and feel. That's why we have to retrain our hearts and minds with Scripture (Romans 12:2). Walking by faith is not an event. It's a *habit*. That's why they call it "walking." It's a *lifestyle* thing. And it takes time and practice.

So what did David do? Did he sink deeper into depression? Did his doubts continue? Did he become bitter, or did he conquer his doubts about God's presence and care? Read for yourself.

> *But I trust in your unfailing love; my heart rejoices in your salvation. I will sing to the Lord, for he has been good to me (Psalm 13:5-6).*

Whoa! What a change! At the beginning of Psalm 13, David is wondering if God has forgotten him forever. He is alone, faithless, and depressed. Now he's proclaiming God's goodness. *Lord, I believe you still love me. I know you'll deliver me. You are so good!* What made the difference? Did David simply plug in a new religious feeling?

Negative.

David was now trusting in a *person*. As a result, his loneliness was replaced by the reality of God's love for him. His sorrow turned to celebration.

Did God feel far away to David? Yes.

Was that feeling rooted in truth? No.

Was God actually far away? Nope.

So what changed David's perspective, and ultimately his feelings? It was a difficult choice to believe the truth that God is always near. He never leaves you. And no matter what happens, that promise will always be true.

Always.

Unfortunately, this doesn't mean we will never again struggle with doubt or feel far from God. Our faith may waver—just as David's did.

But it *does* mean we can be sure that God never leaves us. Even when we feel most alone.

So when your emotions are screaming inside, when circumstances say God doesn't care, you have to make the choice to believe. Your thoughts and emotions may lie to you, but God never will.

And here's your guarantee in writing.

> *I will be with you always... to the very end of the age (Matthew 28:20).*

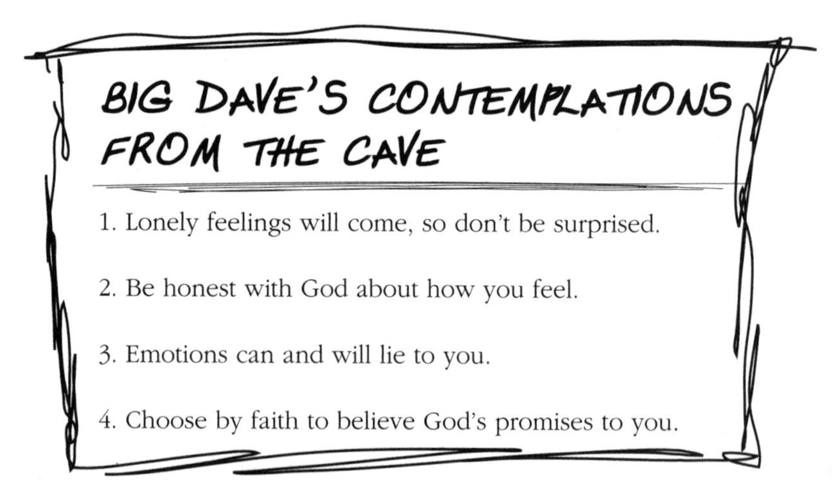

BIG DAVE'S CONTEMPLATIONS FROM THE CAVE

1. Lonely feelings will come, so don't be surprised.

2. Be honest with God about how you feel.

3. Emotions can and will lie to you.

4. Choose by faith to believe God's promises to you.

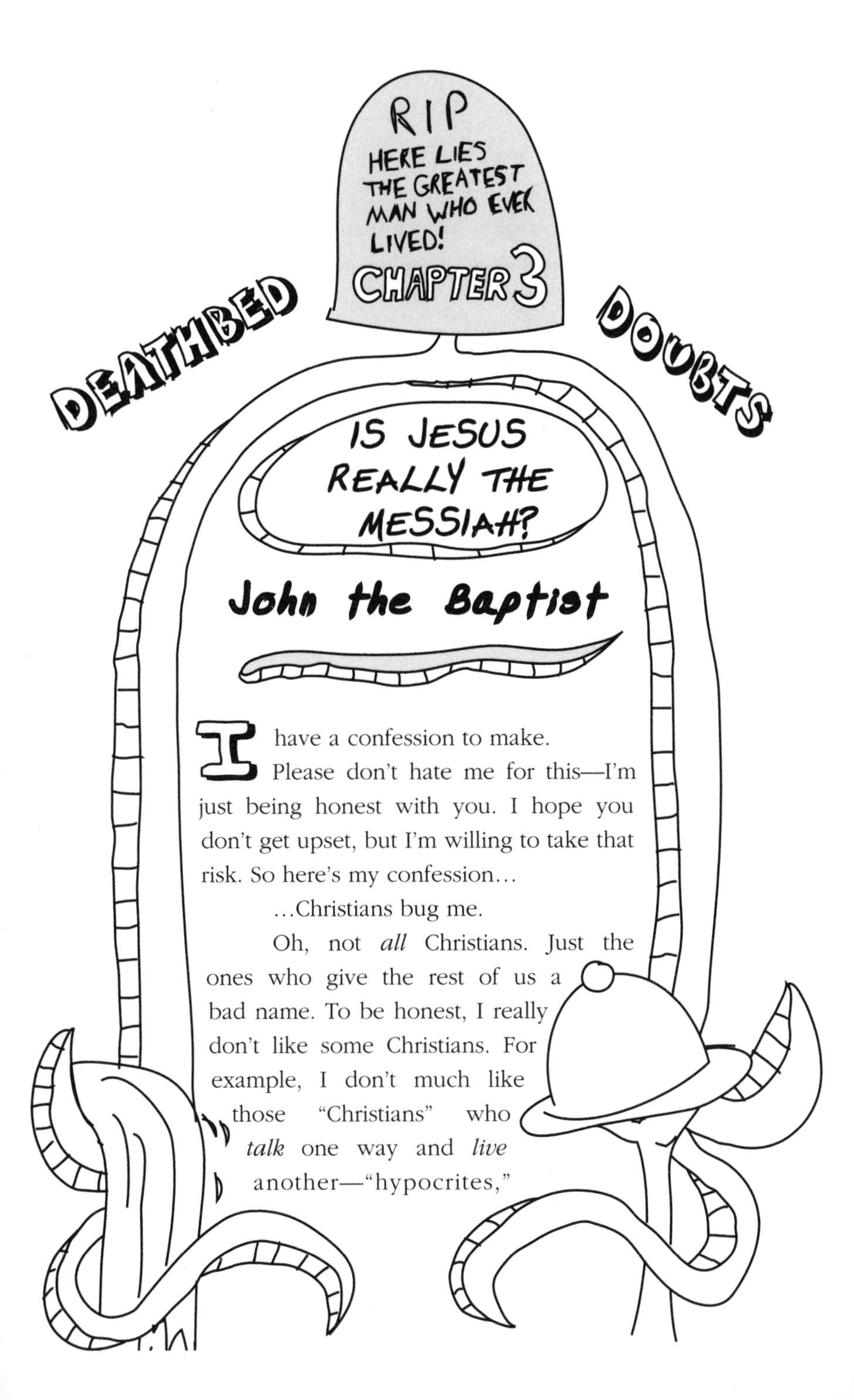

CHAPTER 3

DEATHBED DOUBTS

IS JESUS REALLY THE MESSIAH?

John the Baptist

I have a confession to make.

Please don't hate me for this—I'm just being honest with you. I hope you don't get upset, but I'm willing to take that risk. So here's my confession…

…Christians bug me.

Oh, not *all* Christians. Just the ones who give the rest of us a bad name. To be honest, I really don't like some Christians. For example, I don't much like those "Christians" who *talk* one way and *live* another—"hypocrites," they're called. Then there are the rigid rule-keepers, those who are so concerned with telling the rest of us what we *shouldn't* do that they've lost the beauty of Christianity. They've forgotten what makes our faith so attractive and irresistible to others.

There's one more segment of the Christian population that *really* gets under my skin. It's those well-meaning folks so obsessed with making converts that they end up "overselling the product." They promise things the Gospel doesn't. Often, they talk about the right things—happiness, peace, power for living, forgiveness, abundant life, and fulfillment—but in a way that misleads people. For example, while God does forgive you when you become a Christian, that doesn't mean everyone else will. God forgets your sinful past, but you may still suffer some consequences of it. Yes, you now have abundant life, but that doesn't mean you won't have any more problems. And I think Christians who go around telling others that God will take away all their problems sometimes do more harm than good.

Bottom line: Giving your heart to God *will* improve your life, giving you purpose here and preparation for the hereafter. But you may experience some opposition, hardship, and even persecution. In other words, it won't always be fun. That's what some Christians forget to say when they're witnessing.

For 2,000 years it's been hard to be a Christian. There's been more persecution than prosperity. More hardship than health. More ridicule than riches. Even today, following Christ can mean life is difficult, awkward, embarrassing, and sometimes downright unpleasant. That's because often there's conflict between our faith and our world. When you experience pain and problems—when it's not fun to be a disciple of Jesus—you may start rethinking your faith. That's when the doubts and questions come.

Being a Christian doesn't mean life always goes your way. You and I aren't protected from life's potholes. We're not exempt from suffering, sickness, and death. We don't always get delivered from flat tires and failed tests and other trials that are pretty trivial. We also aren't exempt from car wrecks, family conflicts, financial struggles, and failure. Unexpected hardships show up at your door, rattling your belief system, causing you to question even the most basic elements of your faith.

When this happens, you have two options: 1) chuck your beliefs like a used candy wrapper, or 2) start wrestling with the "uncomfortableness" of your faith. It doesn't matter what church you attend, what Bible translation you use, or how godly your parents are. Somewhere along the way God will fail to meet your expectations. When that happens, it's time to look for some answers.

BILLY GRAHAM MEETS ROB ZOMBIE

Case in point: There was this guy named John, or "John the Baptist," as he is popularly known. We call him John the Baptist because his name was John and he "baptized" people (brilliant, right?). Hmm...how can I describe John to you? Well, think of what you would get if you crossed Rob Zombie with Billy Graham. Scary thought, I know. The result would be a longhaired, half-crazed wild man preaching the Gospel. But let's back up and get a little more specific than that, shall we?

John was the son of a priest named Zechariah and his wife, Elizabeth, who were both descendants of Aaron's priestly line. They were godly people—meaning they were *upright* without being *uptight*. One day, while Zechariah performed his priestly duties, the angel Gabriel appeared to him, announcing that he and Elizabeth would be having a son. This qualified for the bizarre headlines of the day because Zechariah and his wife were "grandparent" age by now. Of course, Gabriel knew this, so to prove his prophecy was true, he made Zechariah a mute until the baby was born.

Gabriel predicted that this child would be "great in the sight of the Lord" (Luke 1:15). The boy was never to cut his hair or drink alcohol. Instead, he would be filled with the Holy Spirit from the day he was born. Preaching in the spirit and power of Elijah, he would prepare the way for the Messiah.

In time, this prophecy came true. Elizabeth got her baby and Zechariah got his voice back. John grew up near Jesus—in fact, they were cousins. But at about age 30, John left home to begin preaching in the wilderness. Like many evangelists today, he

- had a "different" look,
- had only one sermon, and
- delivered it well.

In fact, John's message could be summed up in one word: REPENT!

You can imagine that this made him an unpopular figure, especially with the religious leaders. In short, he was telling Israel's spiritual leaders that *they* needed to get right with God. That kind of preaching wouldn't win him any bonus points with the establishment. But surprisingly, huge crowds came to hear John in the wilderness. And what did they see? A man dressed in camel's hair and a leather belt. In his lunchbox were wild grasshoppers and wild honey. Remember, he hadn't cut his hair in 30 years (and there was no shampoo or conditioner in those days). Combine his wild appearance, wild diet, and one-point sermon, and you've got one bizarre dude. But though he looked like a burned-out-leftover-hippie-from-Woodstock, John was actually an intelligent and humble man. His motto was, "Jesus must become greater and I must become less" (John 3:30).

Good slogan, huh?

One day, while John is baptizing folks in the Jordan River, he sees Jesus. John calls out, "Look, the Lamb of God, who takes away the sin of the world" (John 1:29). Jesus asks John to baptize him and then spends 40 days fasting in the wilderness. After this, Jesus begins his public ministry of teaching and healing throughout

Galilee. John goes back to baptizing and preaching, telling Israel to receive the Messiah who has come.

CALLING A LIFELINE

John's preaching eventually got him into trouble. (Gee, what a surprise.) Here's what happened: King Herod married his brother's wife, Herodias. John told Herod to his face that this was sin. This proved to be a politically incorrect statement. Royally ticked off, Herodias persuaded Herod to arrest John. Herod didn't really want to do this, but as the old saying goes, "If momma ain't happy, ain't nobody happy." So John was locked up in a Roman jail cell for almost two years. John had plenty of time to think during those years, and that's when the wheels began turning in his mind.

> *John's disciples told him about all these things [Jesus had done]. Calling two of them, he sent them to the Lord to ask, "Are you the one who was to come, or should we expect someone else?"*
>
> *When the men came to Jesus, they said, "John the Baptist sent us to you to ask, 'Are you the one who was to come, or should we expect someone else?'" (Luke 7:18-21)*

It's as if John said to himself: "Wait a minute! I've been screaming to everybody that Jesus is the Messiah. But if that's true, why doesn't he deliver me from this prison? I mean, he's heard about my imprisonment. Wait!

What if he's powerless to do anything about it? If so, then maybe he's not the Messiah after all. I am so confused!"

Think of it from John's perspective. He'd spent his entire life preparing the way for Jesus—a lifetime spent in sacrifice, hardship, and selflessly pointing others to the Messiah...and *this* was his reward? So the Baptizer starts wondering if Jesus is the real deal, or just another prophet like himself leading up to the true Messiah.

What about you? Have you ever entertained the thought that whispers: *What if God's not real? What if everything I believe is just made up? What if it's a big hoax, a trick invented by old people to give us hope?* These are what I call "dungeon doubts"—when life causes your faith to be suspect. Don't run from those doubts or ignore them. Like John, face them and work through your tough questions.

John didn't doubt there was going to be a Messiah. He was just wondering out loud if Jesus was the one. 'Cause if he was, then why was his #1 messenger locked up on death row in a dark dungeon? If this really was the "good news" the world had been waiting for, then why did the news keep getting worse for John? If following Christ really was the best way to live, then why was John experiencing so much pain and persecution because of it?

No one was more dedicated to Christ or to his cause. John was a witnessing machine. John was "the man," a rock of righteousness. And yet, in the end, even *he* wondered whether Jesus was the Christ, proving that doubt isn't just for young believers. No matter how mature you are in the Lord, no matter how long you've been a Christian, you *never* stop being human. We all have the potential to doubt, especially during life's dark hours.

Even John the Baptist had fragile faith.

John knew his days were numbered. At any moment, his head would be served up on a platter like a Thanksgiving turkey. Before dying, he had to know if all his trouble was worth it. Following Jesus wasn't turning out as he had imagined. Did his life really have purpose, or would he go down as one of history's biggest failures?

"I SEE DEAD PEOPLE"

Though many of us have had the same thoughts and questions John had, we often keep our questions to ourselves, afraid of being ridiculed or condemned. Not John. He verbalized his dangerous questions. In fact, he sent them straight to Jesus. And so should you. Why? Because of the way Jesus responded to John's doubts. Take a look:

> *At that very time Jesus cured many who had diseases, sicknesses and evil spirits, and gave sight to many who were blind. So he replied to the messengers, "Go back and report to John what you have seen and heard: the blind receive sight, the lame walk, those who have leprosy are cured, the deaf hear, the dead are raised, and the good news is preached to the poor. Blessed is the man who does not fall away on account of me." (Luke 7:21-23)*

Jesus didn't condemn John for his doubts, and neither will he condemn you. There is no rebuke. No *"C'mon, John! What's the matter with you, man? You should never doubt me. Bad boy! You're in deep trouble with God now."* On the contrary, in his humanity, Jesus actually understood John's dilemma. Later, in Gethsemane, Jesus would wonder if God had any other plan to save the world besides the awful cross. Jesus understood John's frailty (and he understands *our* frailty), because Jesus was 100 percent human.

Jesus didn't ignore John's questions. Instead, he responded to them head-on, encouraging John to see, hear, listen, and *believe*. Jesus wanted John to consider what he had *done*—how he had made the blind see, the lame walk, the deaf hear, the dead rise, and the lepers clean. Jesus preached the Gospel to the poor. Being a prophet, John knew those were things Isaiah prophesied that the Messiah would do (Isaiah 35:5; 61:1). Jesus performed miracles, things not explained by human power or persuasion. His works couldn't be written off as some kind of "Galilean hypnotic trance." These were radical changes that couldn't be attributed simply to a positive mental attitude (especially people being raised from the dead!).

YOU'RE GETTING SLEEPY

Jesus *changed lives.*

John was given evidence of *who Jesus was* through miracles that had happened recently. Though it's important to share what God has done for us in the past, it's what he's doing right now that people need to hear. And what are these modern-day miracles? What's the present-day equivalent of lepers being cleansed and dead people coming back to life? What is God's convincing miracle to *your* generation? How can your friends (and you) know for sure that Jesus is still the Messiah? In one word: *change*.

Sure, the historical evidence for Christianity is important...even necessary. But many people in your generation—in every generation—need more than just history, facts, and intellectual evidence. They need living proof that Jesus is alive.

While God still does miracles in our world today, it appears that miraculous signs and wonders are not his main method to win people to himself. I mean, how many times has your school witnessed a river being parted or seen a dead person brought back to life?

NO SMALL CHANGE

When John sought proof that Jesus was the Messiah, Jesus offered him the evidence of changed lives. What kind of change is evidence of God's work in our lives and our world?

 It is *visible* change. People see the difference.

- It is *lasting* change. The change God brings is not merely the result of turning over a new leaf or making a New Year's resolution. The change is permanent—more than just a passing fad or emotional phase.

- It is *complete* change. In other words, God's change isn't just an outward thing. It is an inside job, too.

> Anyone can get a makeover or change their behavior. Not just anyone can be remade into a new creation (2 Corinthians 5:17). Only God can make that kind of change.

But God still provides plenty of evidence of lives that are changing because of him. When John had questions and doubts, Jesus told him to take a look at what was happening in the world when people met him. Jesus was bringing change—change that was visible, long-lasting, and complete.

And God is still bringing this change to people, regardless of race, economic background, or social status.

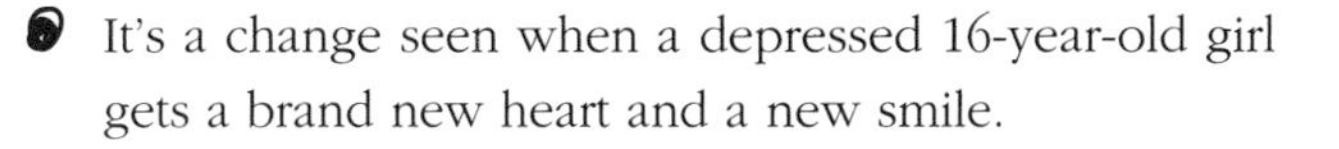

- It's a change seen when a depressed 16-year-old girl gets a brand new heart and a new smile.
- It's a change seen when a teenage boy stops rebelling against his parents.
- It's a change seen when despair dissolves and hope is born in its place.
- It's a change seen when love overcomes anger.
- It's a change seen when bitterness is snuffed out by forgiveness.
- It's a change seen when just surviving is replaced by a life full of purpose and meaning.
- Have you seen these changes in others? Have you experienced such changes? Do others see a difference in you?

Hey, God's not out to make you *religious*. He wants to do more than just make you a moral person. Plenty of religions can do that for you. Instead, God wants to give you a story to tell your world. A story about *life*. Your generation needs to see God's power through a real human life—*yours*.

PARTY FAVOR

Dateline: 29 AD. It's Herod's birthday, and the king throws himself a huge party. In attendance are the most powerful and influential men of Galilee. For entertainment, his stepdaughter dances for the guests. Herod is so pleased with her performance that he offers her anything she wants, up to half his kingdom. After consulting with her mother, Herodias, the daughter makes her request: "I want you to give me the head of John the Baptist…on a platter…right now!"

Stunned and visibly disturbed by the request, Herod nevertheless gives in to keep from losing face in front of his friends (Matthew 14:1-12; Mark 6:14-29). He immediately gives the order to have John's head removed. Still dripping with blood, the head appears minutes later and is presented to Herodias.

When Jesus heard about this, he became very upset and went away by himself to grieve. The Lord really loved John. He knew more than anyone how important John's life and ministry had been. John was a selfless man—all he ever cared about was introducing people to Jesus. And that dedication made a huge impression on Jesus' heart, moving him to call John "more than a prophet" and "the greatest man who ever lived" (Matthew 11:9,11). How would you like that quotation engraved on your tombstone?

> *"Here Lies the Greatest Person Who Ever Lived"*
> *—Jesus Christ*

Not a bad epitaph for a man who never owned more than the clothes on his back. Not bad for a man who, after years of unflinching dedication to Jesus, was hit by a tidal wave of doubt in his final days. But the Good Shepherd, Jesus, gently guided John through those doubts, giving him many *living reasons* to believe. And he'll do the same for you. Jesus didn't oversell himself or shy away from acknowledging the not-so-fun side effects of being his follower. But as John discovered, the benefits far outweigh the sacrifices.

So if you, or anyone you know, ever wonder if Jesus really is the Messiah, and the only way to heaven, then consider what he's done—then and now. Examine the evidence of lives he's changed. Take a look around you at all those living reasons to believe.

Better yet, to see another one of those living reasons, maybe you could just go look in the mirror.

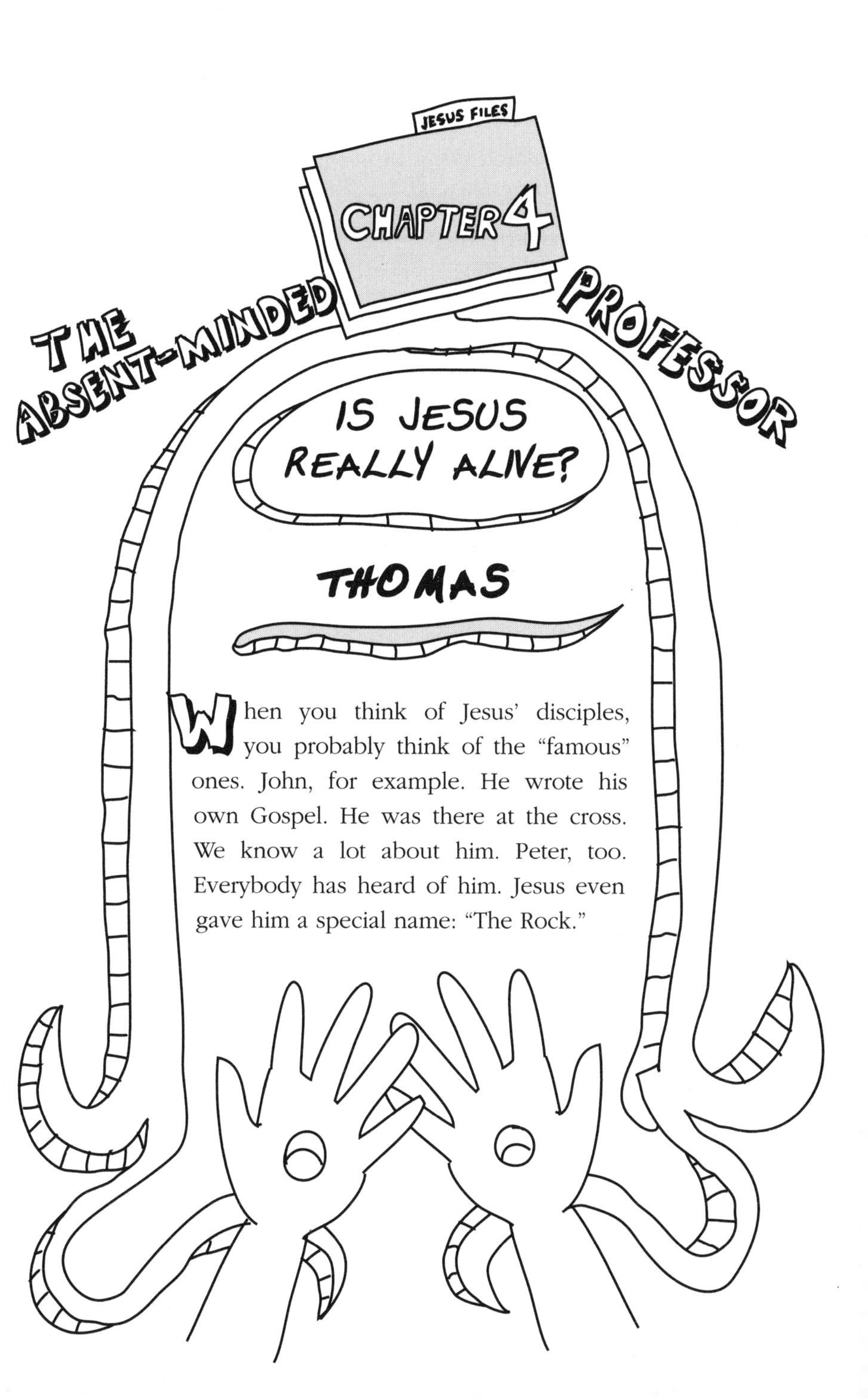

When you think of Jesus' disciples, you probably think of the "famous" ones. John, for example. He wrote his own Gospel. He was there at the cross. We know a lot about him. Peter, too. Everybody has heard of him. Jesus even gave him a special name: "The Rock."

Peter and John are kind of famous in the disciple department. So is Thomas. He's famous for something, too. You may remember him as the guy who refused to believe Jesus was alive unless he saw him with his own eyes.

That's Thomas, a.k.a. "*doubting* Thomas." For two centuries, Thomas (or "Didymus") has been tattooed with this loser label, even though we've forgiven the other disciples' failures and faults. I mean, we don't call them "*denying* Peter," "*ambitious* James," or "*stupid* Phillip." But Thomas got stuck with a bummer of a nickname. As such, his reputation has suffered. He's the "bad boy" of the Twelve because he demanded proof Jesus was alive. Since 30 AD, we've focused on his single moment of doubt, ignoring years of devotion to Christ.

Maybe it's time to re-examine the evidence.

C.S.I.

Let's take a few minutes to dust off Thomas' case file and see if there are clues indicating that Thomas may have been falsely convicted, or at least accused of the wrong crime. Let's conduct our own "crime scene investigation." Here are the key questions in the case of the Doubting Disciple:

- Did Thomas get a bad rap?
- Has history been fair to him?
- Was his "doubt" really as bad as it sounds?
- Was there more to his life?
- Why was he so skeptical that day?
- Is there evidence the other disciples might have had doubts about Jesus' resurrection?

Rewind the video back to Jesus' last night with his disciples. They've just finished a meal together (the Last Supper) where Jesus gave them final instructions before his death. Of course, they still didn't get that Jesus was about to be crucified. Following dinner, he led them to their favorite prayer spot a little garden outside Jerusalem called Gethsemane.

Once there, Jesus became overwhelmed with grief and stress. That's because he knew something the disciples didn't. He knew he was about to get hit by a torture train.

Jesus knew all about crucifixion, no doubt having witnessed scores of them growing up under a cruel Roman government. But that wasn't what was on his mind. Don't misunderstand. He didn't look forward to being crucified. It's just that something far worse was waiting for him. He knew that in going to the cross he would experience the punishment for all of humanity's sin. On the cross the Father would completely forsake him, abandoning him to a black existence only those now in hell experience. He understood the Father would unleash an eternity's worth of wrath and torture on his soul. That was (and still is) the punishment for sin. It's what is waiting for people without Christ the moment they draw their last breath.

Faced with shouldering that enormous burden for you and me, Jesus gathered his closest companions around him. In the garden, he asked them to watch and pray while he knelt to pour out his heart to God. A short time later, Judas and his "new friends" showed up. A small skirmish broke out, and Jesus was arrested. Eventually he was tried, convicted, and crucified. Frightened by the prospect of a similar fate, the disciples scattered like mice in a roomful of cats. Except for Peter and John, the disciples

ran for the hills and hid, trembling with fear behind locked doors. And they stayed there all weekend.

Jesus was dead. Their Messiah had been murdered. The Son of God had been butchered, callously nailed to a cross. And just in case anyone was wondering, that officially meant "game over" for the Jesus thing. The End. Finished. Terminated. Roll credits. There would be none of this "kingdom" Christ had spoken of so many times.

The dream was over.

Even so, the heat was still on the disciples. They had to lay low for a while until things cooled down. If the Jewish leaders and Roman officials meant to crush this new spiritual revolution, then crucifying its leader would be a good way to accomplish that goal. And if you were a disciple, popping your head up out of the underground at this point just might mean getting it chopped off by a Roman sword. It might even get you crucified. So you can sort of understand why Jesus' followers weren't staging any "See You at the Cross" rallies. No way. Self-preservation immediately became the flavor of the month. It was time to be invisible.

MISSING PERSONS

That Sunday evening, a secret meeting of the Twelve was called. We're not exactly sure why they met, but we know ten of them were present (Judas had killed himself, and Thomas was nowhere to be found).

Maybe they gathered to try to make sense of all this. Maybe it was time for one of those "What do we do now?" huddles. Maybe they just wanted to take a head count to see who was still alive!

It's more likely that they gathered to discuss an unbelievable rumor that Jesus had risen from the dead. Some of the women had started the rumor, but the men weren't buying their story. Today, we'd diagnose those women as suffering from "Post-Cross Traumatic Stress Syndrome." Men didn't view women with high regard in those days.

Whatever their reason for meeting that night, Thomas wasn't there. And when you're a small group, you always notice when someone is missing. Then, while they were gathered, Jesus showed up! More alive than ever, he invited the ten disciples to examine the evidence of his resurrection. John put it this way:

On the evening of that first day of the week, when the disciples were together, with the doors locked for fear of the Jews, Jesus came and stood among them and said, "Peace be with you!" After he said this, he showed them his hands and side. The disciples were overjoyed when they saw the Lord...

Now Thomas (called Didymus), one of the Twelve, was not with the disciples when Jesus came. So the other disciples told him, "We have seen the Lord!"

But he said to them, "Unless I see the nail marks in his hands and put my finger where the nails were, and put my hand into his side, I will not believe it." (John 20:19-20, 24-25)

This vivid scene teaches us a life principle we can sink our teeth into. Here it is: *When God's people come together, God shows up.* But there's an obvious catch: *If you're not there, you won't experience it.*

In other words, when you miss the fellowship, you miss the dynamic of God's presence among believers. Now that's a new way of looking at youth group and church, isn't it? Imagine if you believed God was going to show up at church. I don't think anyone would have to drag you out of bed by your ankles on Sunday mornings. Think how exciting it would be if your church expected Jesus to *be there* when you worshipped him.

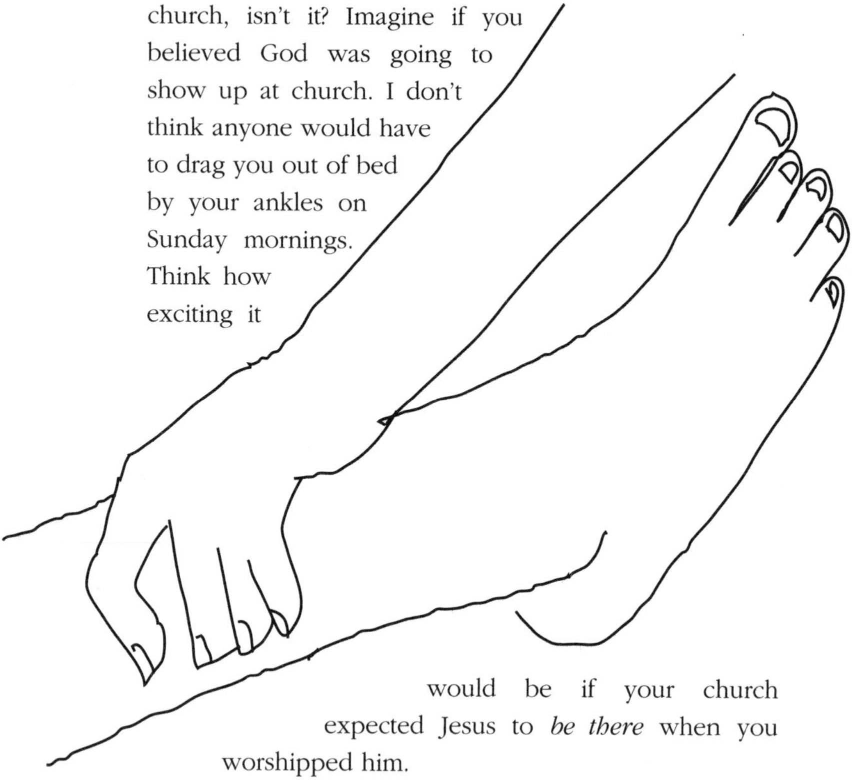

I'm not saying God isn't with you when you're alone. There are awesome times of personal worship when it's just you and God. But we're talking about something else here. Something very different happens when Christians gather to worship. As you read your New Testament, you discover the majority of it is addressed to groups of believers rather than individuals. That's because God never meant for us to walk the Christian life by ourselves. Instead, we were designed to be interdependent. As the author of Hebrews writes, *Let us not give up meeting together, as some are in the habit of doing, but let us encourage one another—and all the more as you see the Day approaching*. (Hebrews 10:25)

GOD IN THE HERE AND NOW

God is waiting for us when we come together in his name. Scripture tells us we really need the body of Christ. He wants us to experience what it means to be a part of his family. It's when we're together that we receive

- Equipping from God's Word
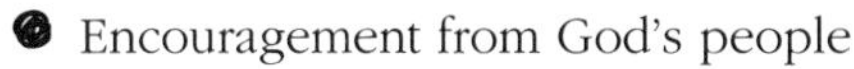
- Encouragement from God's people
- Enjoyment of God's presence

When we're together, we get something we can't get when we're alone. We experience the "bigness" of God through fellowship, group celebration, corporate prayer, and seeing needs met. When God's family gathers, it's not to prove to the world Jesus is alive. Seekers and even skeptical unbelievers are always welcome, accepted, and loved, and we should be sensitive to their needs. But reaching others is not the number one reason we have "church."

The number one reason Christians gather as church is to experience God!

The question is not, "Does the world believe in God?" The real question is, "Do *Christians* really believe he's alive?" Do we believe that where two or more are gathered in his name, he's actually among us? Of course, God *is* everywhere, but he's not *made known* or *experienced* everywhere. His presence should be experienced when Christians come together.

If that's true, what does it look like in a group of present-day disciples? How would your youth ministry be different if Jesus "showed up" each week? We might look at the example of the first church for some help here. What did their "youth group" look like? Check out what Luke witnessed and recorded in Acts 2:42-47:

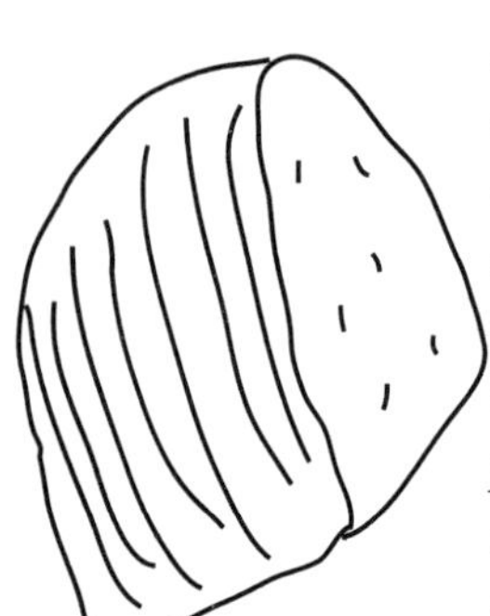

> *They devoted themselves to the apostles' teaching and to the fellowship, to the breaking of bread and to prayer. Everyone was filled with awe, and many wonders and miraculous signs were done by the apostles. All the believers were together and had everything in common. Selling their possessions and goods, they gave to anyone as he had need. Every day they continued to meet together in the temple courts. They broke bread in their homes and ate together with glad and sincere hearts, praising God and enjoying the favor of all the people. And the Lord added to their number daily those who were being saved.*

Every church today has its own distinct personality. But there are some characteristics of that first church in Jerusalem that should be true for all churches, regardless of location, age, or denomination. Let's take a look at a few of them.

1. *They wanted to hear from God.* When the first Christians met together, there was a hunger to hear God speak. Of course, there were no Bibles, so the apostles taught them. And we're not talking some dull speaker or a boring Bible study. Believe me, I've been put to sleep by some of the worst speakers. Jesus gave God's Word to his disciples in interesting ways—ways that made sense to them (John 17:6-8). Through hearing God's truth in a language that makes sense to you, your understanding of God and the Christian life becomes more clear and "livable." The early church gathered to hear God speak, just as the disciples gathered on the evening of that first Easter. Thomas missed the fellowship that night—and missed hearing from Jesus.

2. *They wanted to talk to God.* The early church didn't meet just to hear from God. Their hearts overflowed back to him as well. Through group prayer, they brought all their concerns and needs to him. Through worship, they praised him. Uniting their hearts this way, they experienced the powerful presence of God. They also regularly remembered Christ's sacrifice for them through the Lord's Supper.

3. *They were committed to one another.* Jesus told his followers that one thing above all else would show the world they were truly his disciples. What was it? Well, it wasn't their Christian T-shirts, youth buildings, or the ability to quote the book of Amos with one arm tied behind

their backs. Instead, it was something much cooler than that. Jesus said their *love for one another* would convince others they belonged to him (John 13:35). In other words, the world will know God is real (that he's really here) if Christians show love to each other, even during hard times. For that first "youth group," love meant

- Spending time together (at church and in homes)
- A common focus (loving Christ)
- Sacrificing to meet each other's needs (material or spiritual)

As soldiers in battle, the early followers of Jesus were determined that nobody got left behind. And nobody did. Empty stomachs were filled, debts were paid, broken hearts were mended, and every need was met. In short, church was a very good place to be. No wonder people were joining by the hundreds! Duh! Where else in the world were you going to find people who genuinely loved and cared for you like that?

As for Thomas, his greatest need in life was to see the risen Christ. But because he chose to be somewhere else, he missed it, and his need wasn't met.

I don't believe Thomas' crime was that he was an *evil doubter*. Think about it. Considering all that had happened to them that weekend, would *you* have believed it if someone told you Jesus had suddenly come back from the grave? I can see how that story might be a bit hard to swallow.

No, Thomas' struggle wasn't really with doubt. His problem was not devoting himself to the body of Christ when he really needed it. Instead of "doubting Thomas," maybe he should have been labeled "disappearing Didymus."

The same principle applies to us today. Unless we're convinced we really need our brothers and sisters at church, we'll never be motivated to see God meet with us when we *do* come together.

Shannon was one of those motivated people. Though only 5'2", she stood tall for Christ at her school and took a lot of heat for her faith. Other students made fun of her, intimidated, and even threatened her—and she shed quite a few tears over that abuse. But she never flinched or backed down, remaining strong through high school and college.

My most vivid memory of Shannon is seeing her walk through our youth-room door on Wednesday nights. With arms raised high and a Texas-sized smile, she'd let out a cheer celebrating her arrival "back home" again. After being a social punching bag at school all week, she could hardly wait to get to the place where she found security, acceptance, love, and friendship. She always expected God to show up and meet with us. And he did. For Shannon, church was more than a *place*. It was *people*. Many people in love with the same One.

Thomas' big blunder was flying solo that day. He picked the wrong day to miss youth group.

"OH, MY GOD!"

One week after the "doubting episode," Jesus again appeared to his disciples as they met. And this time, Thomas was there. Here's how it went down:

A week later his disciples were in the house again, and Thomas was with them. Though the doors were locked, Jesus came and stood among them and said, "Peace be with you!"

Then he said to Thomas, "Put your finger here; see my hands. Reach out your hand and put it into my side. Stop doubting and believe."

Thomas said to him, "My Lord and my God!"

Then Jesus told him, "Because you have seen me, you have believed; blessed are those who have not seen and yet have believed." (John 20:26-29)

Can you imagine the look on Thomas' face when Jesus suddenly appeared? Picture the other disciples nodding their heads as if to say, "*We told you so, dude!*" And though Jesus invited Thomas to touch him and be fully convinced he was real, there's no indication Thomas ever did so. Instead, Thomas believed and confessed Christ as his Lord and God (probably bowing before him). Betcha anything Thomas didn't miss church the next week.

So how can *you* experience the presence of God in your youth group and church—even when others don't?

FIRST, *be there*. Show up at church faithfully. Make it your priority. There will always be something else you could be doing (homework, practice, TV, friends, work, etc.). But honor God with your faithfulness to him.

SECOND, *be committed*. Your brothers and sisters in Christ have something you need (and vice versa). Even if you feel you have little in common with them, concentrate on all that you share in Christ. Get involved in their lives.

THIRD, *be expectant*. When you hear God's Word taught, expect him to speak to you. As you worship, anticipate him filling the room along with your praises. Do this, and you'll experience the presence of the risen Christ.

If Thomas had stayed close to his spiritual family, he would have seen the risen Jesus with his own eyes. He wasn't there with the other disciples in the locked room. But that doesn't make him a life-long loser. It certainly doesn't mean he deserves to be "doubting Thomas" for eternity. He learned his lesson, so let's give him a break, okay?

Jesus is alive, friend. And he's there when those personally touched by him come together to honor him.

Hey, do you have a youth group? If so, do you believe you really need those teenagers at church? Are you faithful to that group? Or has your church filed a missing person's report on you?

Is church a safety net for you? A lifeline? Will you expect God to speak this week? Are you ready to conquer your doubts with Jesus' presence? Will you bow and say with Thomas, "My Lord and my God"?

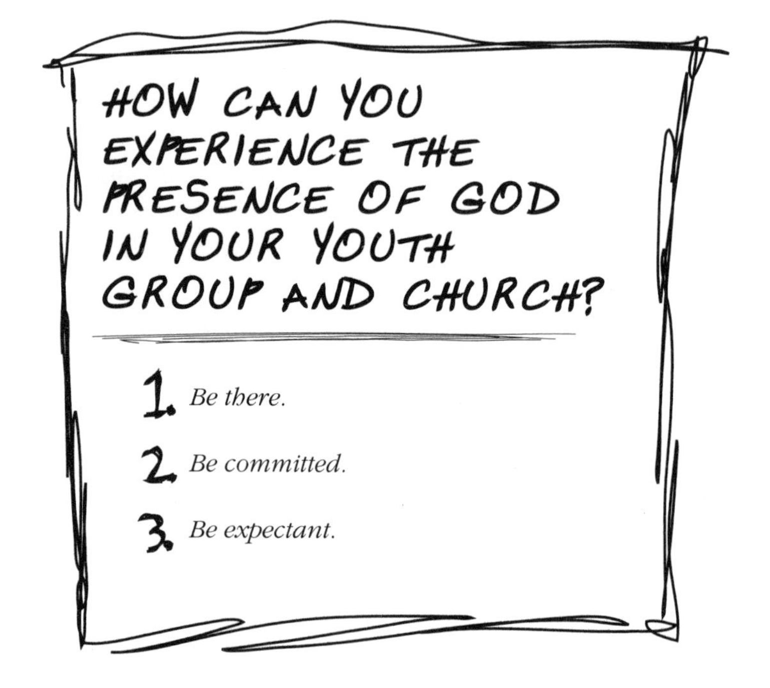
HOW CAN YOU EXPERIENCE THE PRESENCE OF GOD IN YOUR YOUTH GROUP AND CHURCH?
1. Be there.
2. Be committed.
3. Be expectant.

FAITHFUL FAILURES:

ENCOURAGEMENT FROM SCRIPTURE'S OVERCOMERS

What would you do if you were the richest person alive? What if you possessed everything your heart desired? Whatever your fantasy, it happened. We're talking the world at your fingertips. More cash than time to spend it. Mega-celebrity status. Living in luxury. Sound too good to be true? Nah, it's all real, and it happened to a man named Solomon. He was a guy who *saw* it all, *had* it all, and *did* it all. Nothing was beyond his reach, including houses, money, servants, yachts, cars (oops...horses), and women.

Yet even with all these things, Solomon realized he was still searching for something more. He asked the same questions people are asking today:

Who am I?

What's my purpose in life?

Do I matter?

The Bible says Solomon was also the wisest man who ever lived, but he still lacked something. His life felt incomplete, like a puzzle with a missing piece. So with an explorer's spirit, he determined to find that missing piece...and he let us tag along for the ride. When Solomon set out on a personal expedition, he recorded his observations about life in his journal, Ecclesiastes.

Of course, King Solomon was the original "Joe Billionaire." He had the finances to pursue and purchase whatever his eyes desired (Ecclesiastes 2:8). You don't have Solomon's bucks, so you can't personally retrace his steps. However, you can still discover what he learned in his search by reading his journal. This way, you can hang out with a guy who's been around the block a few times, someone who's qualified to show you what life is really all about. Think of it as "life lessons from a 5,000-year-old man." These are Solomon's "Road Rules," outlined for you in four easy-to-understand categories:

- Observations: What I *Saw*
- Pursuits: What I *Did*
- Conclusions: What I *Decided*
- Benefits: What I *Gained*

WHAT I SAW

Before leaving the driveway on his epic journey, Solomon paused to make a few general observations about life. Look them up in your Bible and see if you think they're still true today.

OBSERVATION 1: PEOPLE COME, PEOPLE GO (1:1-4).

What's the purpose of life? Solomon wonders. You're here, then you're gone. You're born, then you go through infancy, childhood, adolescence, adulthood, old age, and finally you die. And for what? Every old person you see was once 17 and thought he'd be young forever. Now he's slowly sliding toward death. Our existence on earth seems like a meaningless cycle, going nowhere. Life is nothing more than a series of births and funerals, with everything in between *meaningless*.

OBSERVATION 2: NATURE IS SPINNING ITS WHEELS, TOO (1:5-7).

There's no real progress in nature. The sun and moon keep moving, but they never get anywhere! What's up with that? It's all just monotonous futility. There's no point to our crummy existence on this planet or to the planet itself. *Meaningless!*

Thousands of years later, in his book *A History of Europe,* H.A.L. Fisher wrote: "One intellectual excitement has been denied me. Men wiser than I have discovered in history a plot, a rhythm, a predetermined plan. But I see only one emergency following another, as wave follows upon wave."

Amen! Solomon would say. *Life is so... so...random.* The only pattern he saw was a meaningless cycle.

OBSERVATION 3: HUMANITY IS NEVER SATISFIED (1:8).

Looking around, Solomon concludes that though we are constantly filling ourselves with things, we are never satisfied! More money. Faster cars. Bigger speakers. Better PCs. More romantic relationships. More friends. More education. A better job. A different husband or wife. It doesn't matter. The "good life" is just an illusion. Nothing satisfies. *Meaningless!*

OBSERVATION 4: THERE'S NOTHING NEW (1:9-10).

Life is b-o-r-i-n-g. It's just the "same ol', same ol'." People still try to be cool. Kids still rebel against their parents. People still invent new ways to try to make themselves happy, thinking they're the first to experience them. But they're the same things people have used for centuries (money, sex, power, intellect, etc.). Everything's the same. Even the sins are the same. They're just packaged differently.

OBSERVATION 5: NOBODY REMEMBERS YOU WHEN YOU'RE GONE (1:11).

What's the point of school? (I'm sure you've asked that before!) Why get a job? Why fall in love? Why have a family? For what? Soon you'll be dead and gone, and who'll really care you were ever here? Your name eventually disappears from your tombstone. And what will it matter that you were present in this emptiness? You're gone, then forgotten.

French novelist André Maurois wrote, "The universe is indifferent. Who created it? Why are we here on this puny mud heap spinning in space? I have not the slightest idea, and I am convinced that no one has the least idea."

Solomon agreed: There's no such thing as a *purpose-driven life* because there is no *purpose*!

So what did he conclude? Life is empty (1:14). At least, that's what his T-shirt said. In other words, life is nothing more than a pointless, trivial, vain, empty, hopeless, depressing, worthless walk in the dark. Living is an exercise in futility, spinning your wheels. It's absurd, so...let's party! Or just end your life now. Just as many young people today, he wondered, *What's the use?*

But even though Solomon acknowledged this emptiness, he reasoned to himself: *How can I be totally sure there's no meaning and happiness in life unless I search for it myself?* So just to be sure, Solomon decided to dive in head first, trying out nine different pursuits in his search for significance.

WHAT I DID

PURSUIT 1: THE "EINSTEIN EFFECT" (1:17)

First, Solomon decided to check out wisdom. In today's world, you could say he studied hard, made good grades, became part of the honor society, aced the ACT, and got a full academic scholarship to college. For a while, he felt good about himself because he was smart, but the feeling soon turned sour. He realized that having all that knowledge only meant he understood even *more* how futile life really was! (1:18). He concluded that it would be better to be ignorant and happy. Scratch wisdom. It's not the answer.

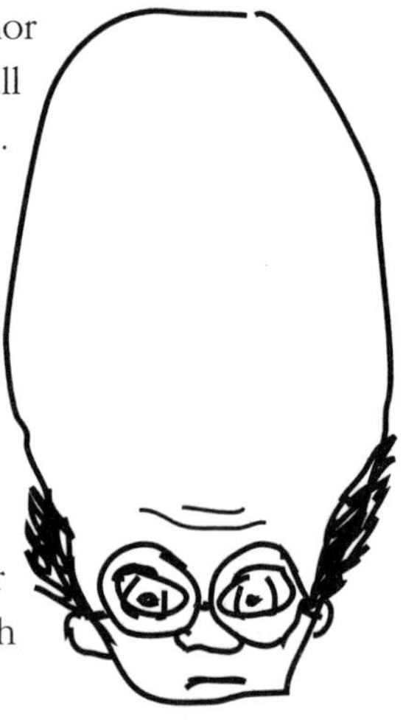

PURSUIT 2: SPRING BREAK FEVER (2:1)

Being smart only gave Solomon a big headache, so he decided to have some fun. He wanted to play, and he found some fellow fun-seekers to join him. Bungee jumping, skydiving, cow tipping, mailbox smashing, mall cruising, movie going, and practical joking. Each thrill was topped by the next one. But all that fun was like cotton candy—great to the taste buds, but no substance. The thrill quickly melted, leaving behind a gnawing feeling in his gut. Besides, all that freedom carried some serious consequences (11:9). Fun just doesn't last. Now the king had a headache *and* a stomachache.

PURSUIT 3: COMEDY CLUB (2:2)

Having fun only made Solomon sad, so to cheer himself up he summoned the best comedians in the world...*all* of them—Adam Sandler, Jim Carrey, Robin Williams, Chris Tucker—they were all there...even the Three Stooges! And the laughter was side-splitting...while it lasted. But when the laughing stopped, his heart was still in pain. Is it any wonder that many of the greatest comedians of our day, by their own admission, are some of the most troubled and unhappy people? Laughter simply can't drown out the misery of life's emptiness. To put it another way, there's nothing funny about an empty life.

PURSUIT 4: BUZZ IN A BOTTLE (2:3)

Still hurting from the emptiness, Solomon decided to numb the pain of his achy-breaky heart with drugs. So he drank...a lot. Waking up each morning from a drunken binge, he found he was more depressed than the night before. And it was starting to take more and more alcohol to give him the same feeling. What's worse, the pain kept coming back when the buzz wore off. Drugs couldn't erase the haunting reality that life on this planet was *nothing*. His point? There is no painkiller for the soul.

PURSUIT 5: THE WORLD IS NOT ENOUGH (2:4-6).

"Okay, *things* then! I just need more *things*!" So Solomon built for himself massive gardens, ponds, and vineyards (to make more wine!). In modern-day terms, he simply bought whatever he wanted—clothes, digital devices,

PCs, PDAs, ipods, laptops, guitars, amps, wave-runners, 4-wheelers, cars, and a house at the beach. But there's only so much time in each day to enjoy all these things, and you have to keep updating your "tech-toys" to stay current. Soon Solomon became a slave to his toys—and that was boring. Once again...*emptiness*. Stuff stinks.

PURSUIT 6: IMAGE IS EVERYTHING (2:7).

Like all people, Solomon wanted to be liked and popular—to be *somebody*. Nothing wrong with that, but consider that Solomon could actually afford to "buy" his admirers. So he did, purchasing slaves to surround him. The more he had, the more important he felt. But as any celebrity will tell you, fame is a fickle friend. When your song drops from the charts, when the roar of the crowd is replaced by the chirping of crickets, or when you declare bankruptcy—see how many friends you still have. See how special you still feel. The whole "image thing" got old. Popularity ain't all it's cracked up to be.

PURSUIT 7: SERIOUS COIN (2:8)

Solomon's cash flow was enormous. In one year, his base income was 25 tons of gold, or approximately $27 million! (1 Kings 10:14). And that's tax-free cash, baby! Have you ever thought that if you just had more money, life would be better? I have! Think of what you could do with all that money. Admittedly, money actually *can* buy lots of good times, but it couldn't give Solomon what he was looking for. He discovered that cash was a counterfeit contentment. Money can't buy you love.

PURSUIT 8: LIFE AT THE PLAYBOY MANSION (2:8)

Solomon next turned to one of the most intoxicating pursuits of all: SEX. He was the original player, dating (and eventually marrying) virtually every girl that caught his eye. And you can bet he wasn't taking them back to the palace for Bible study, either! His lust for sex led him to chase women whose hearts were far from God. And that's where his heart ended up as well. In the end, he collected 700 wives and 300 mistresses (1 Kings 11:1-8). But even though Solomon's sexual fantasies were fulfilled thousands of times over, ironically, he remained unfulfilled. Sex may sell, but outside of God's design, it can't satisfy the deepest longings of the human heart.

PURSUIT 9: IT'S GOOD TO BE THE KING (2:10).

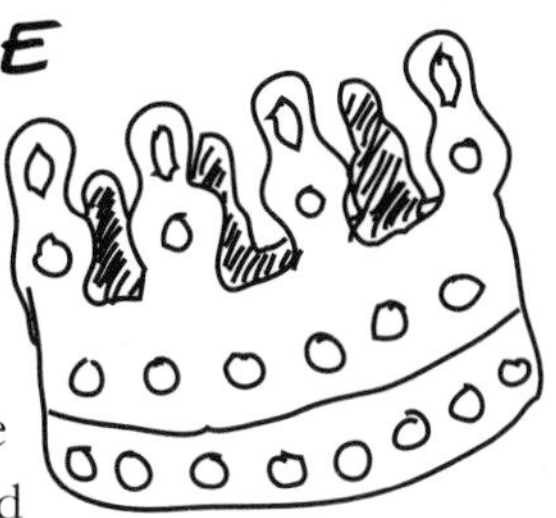

As Israel's king, Solomon possessed a world of influence, and this power made him feel almost like a god. Hmm, sounds familiar (Genesis 3:5). When the king spoke, people jumped and things happened. Like Donald Trump (but with better hair), he could hire, fire, promote, demote, and even *execute*. But being the king of his own empire eventually lost its appeal. It became nothing. His intellect led him to say all that power was like chasing the wind (2:11). And, of course, you can never catch the wind, right?

I'll shoot straight with you. All these things (money, possessions, popularity, sex) *do* give a temporary feeling of fulfillment, importance, and happiness. But they're only cheap substitutes for the real thing. Solomon's soul was like a cup with holes in it—no matter how much he poured in, it kept draining out. He simply couldn't pour fast enough to fill the holes.

WHAT I DECIDED

Solomon finally wised up and plugged in the missing ingredient to his life-size jigsaw puzzle. Rich, handsome, and highly intelligent, he knew all along he was more than flesh, bone, hormones, and hedonism. He knew he was first and foremost a *spiritual* being....with *spiritual* needs. And no amount of mental, physical, or emotional trinkets could plug that hole in his soul.

His three conclusions are the keys to unlocking the door of meaning and happiness for you and me. He's being honest with us here. No more pretending. No sugarcoating. No airbrushing. And don't be fooled by their simplicity. These are true and trustworthy laws of life. They are Solomon's "Road Rules," and they work.

ROAD RULE 1: ENJOY LIFE FULLY (ECCLESIASTES 2:24-25; 3:12; 5:18; 9:7).

"For without him, who can eat or find enjoyment?" Solomon writes. "To the man who pleases him, God gives wisdom, knowledge, and happiness" (2:24-25). Solomon concludes that real, lasting fun, enjoyment, and satisfaction can't be experienced until you bring God into your life equation. True fun is a gift from God because the things you enjoy are things *he* made. And he made them for you to enjoy! You have his permission to enjoy life to the fullest measure! He wants you to experience the best in every day (Ecclesiastes 7:10; 9:10; John 10:10).

Life is meant to be *enjoyed*, not *endured*.

ROAD RULE 2: TAKE GOD SERIOUSLY (ECCLESIASTES 5:1-10; 11:9-10).

Fear isn't always a bad thing. In fact, it can be a very good thing. Fear of losing a game can motivate you to play harder. Fear of flunking a test can motivate you to study more. Fear of getting 4,000 stitches in your face can motivate you to stop at a red light. But fear also has a place in your relationship to God. We all need a healthy fear of God, giving him the reverence and respect he deserves. Solomon remembered that God is God and wisely advised us that having this fear would prevent us from

- Strutting into God's presence (5:1-3).
- Making promises to God that we don't keep (5:4-6).
- Sowing seeds of spiritual rebellion (11:9-10).

You *should* be afraid of living a mediocre, wasted life. Taking God seriously will help you avoid that tragic mistake.

ROAD RULE 3: SEEK GOD EARLY (12:1, 13-14).

Solomon's last rule is a plea straight from his heart to yours. It's a call to action from the wisest man who ever lived:

"Remember your Creator in the days of your youth, before the days of trouble come and the years approach when you will say, 'I find no pleasure in them.'" (12:1)

Remembering your Creator means daily acknowledging his right to rule in your life. It means recognizing God as the one essential ingredient for a happy life. It means you understand that without him, you are merely floating through space…just existing, "chasing the wind." It means you understand how badly you need him.

Notice that Solomon adds the phrase, "in the days of your youth." Why does he say this? Because each of us has a limited amount of time to put God first in our lives. After the teenage years, the human heart typically grows cold and calloused towards spiritual things. "Seize the day," Solomon is saying. "Now is your chance. Now!"

Solomon's Road Rules teach us that the best part of life happens when a relationship with God is our number one pursuit. He's not saying that money, possessions, power, fun, or any of those other things are inherently wrong. But it's only when we put God in charge of those areas that we experience true enjoyment.

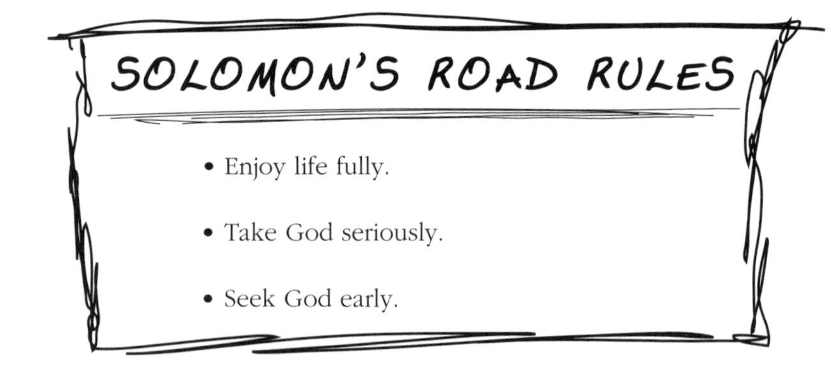

SOLOMON'S ROAD RULES

- Enjoy life fully.
- Take God seriously.
- Seek God early.

WHAT I GAINED

Before letting him go, let's ask Solomon one more question. *Why is it so important to follow your Road Rules?* In other words, *What's in it for us if we enjoy life fully, take God seriously, and seek him right now?*

"Thanks for asking!" Solomon says. *"Following my Road Rules will do several things for you."*

1. YOU'LL SEE LIFE CLEARLY (3:1-11).

Getting your priorities in order causes life to start making sense. This theme runs throughout the Bible. When your priorities are in order, you see more of what life is all about. You get smart, gaining wisdom beyond your years (Psalm 119:99). You're able to interpret life, seeing through the world's lies when others remain blind (2 Corinthians 4:4). Would you like that?

2. YOU'LL DISCOVER YOUR LIFE PURPOSE (3:11-13).

Putting God first will help you find answers to questions everyone is searching for, such as: *Who am I? Why am I here? Why was I created?* Knowing God gives you identity, purpose, mission—a reason to live! God has incredible plans for your life, and as you pursue him, those plans are revealed to you (Jeremiah 9:23-26; Jeremiah 29:11; Romans 12:2).

3. YOU'LL NEVER LOSE HOPE (3:17).

God is fair. He gives every person exactly what he or she deserves. That means no sin goes unpunished. It also means that no good deed goes unrewarded. He misses nothing. So you can have confidence he'll make everything turn out right in the end. Another part of this hope is that he promises to complete the awesome work he began in you at salvation (Philippians 1:6). Knowing this brings peace to your heart and mind (John 14:27; Philippians 4:7). It means all your sacrifices and struggles are worth it! This hope is what keeps you from giving up.

4. YOU'LL ENJOY LASTING HAPPINESS (2:26; 3:22).

Once you see life through God's eyes, you begin experiencing the meaning of life itself, the kind of life he wants you to enjoy. It's a happiness that's not based on what happens to you, but rather one rooted in Christ and your relationship with him. It's this quality of lifestyle that will attract others to him.

Had you bumped into Solomon at a party with a woman on each arm or seen him the morning after an all-night drinking binge, you might have concluded he was a total loser. You might have thought, *What a failure. Earth's wisest man wasting all those years on women, things, and meaningless pursuits. That's not smart. That's dumb!*

"True," Solomon might have responded. "I did pursue things leading to failure and despair. But in the end, I proved to be wise after all, by recognizing the role my Creator deserved in my life."

Maybe you've wondered about sex, money, popularity, possessions, and other subjects Solomon majored in. Or perhaps you've dabbled in them yourself. Maybe you've done more than just dabble.

Either way, Solomon stands in the road, warning you of the pain and disappointment he experienced. Take an honest look at his empty pursuits. Then take a step of faith towards wisdom. Make his Road Rules your own, and enjoy all the benefits that come from that choice.

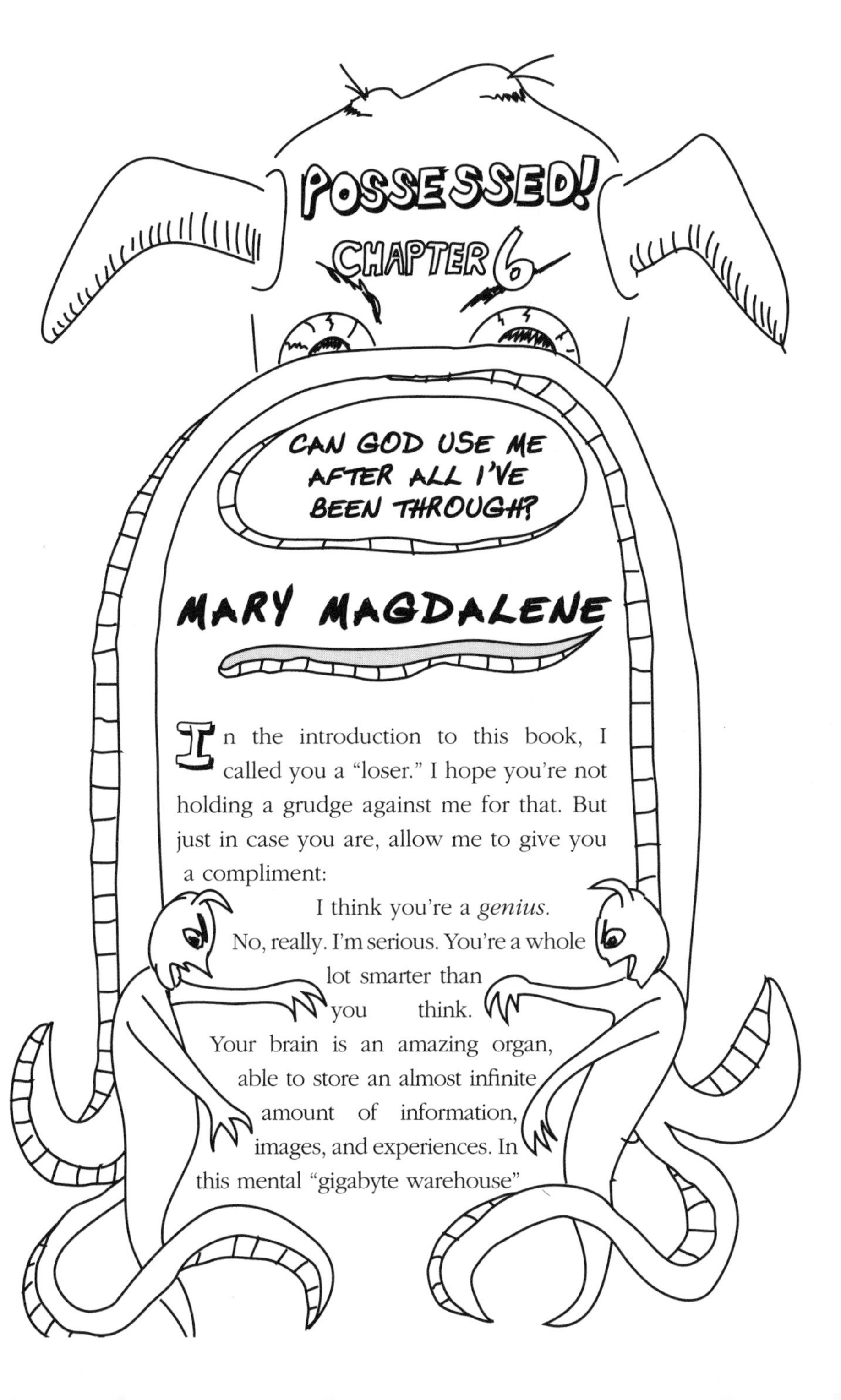

POSSESSED!

CHAPTER 6

CAN GOD USE ME AFTER ALL I'VE BEEN THROUGH?

MARY MAGDALENE

In the introduction to this book, I called you a "loser." I hope you're not holding a grudge against me for that. But just in case you are, allow me to give you a compliment:

I think you're a *genius.*

No, really. I'm serious. You're a whole lot smarter than you think.

Your brain is an amazing organ, able to store an almost infinite amount of information, images, and experiences. In this mental "gigabyte warehouse" is contained virtually every thought and experience you've ever had. And you can access those memories whenever you want, with a connection speed faster than a T-l cable!

Of course, some memories are more vivid than others. Some are like old photographs. Faded over time, they've lost their original color and are hard to recall. Like the time your mom says you threw off your diaper and ran around the front yard naked. And as you get older, your *autobahn* memory system may resemble more of a country road, causing you to experience traffic jams on your brain's information highway. That's why your grandfather sometimes calls you by your cousin's name.

So imagine how tragic it must be to lose your memory through accident or injury. Think of all the great memories you'd lose—video and still images recalling life's greatest moments: the first time you got up on water skis, the feeling of "first love," your favorite Christmas morning, that special birthday or family vacation. These are the happy places in your mind. Memory is a good thing.

On the other hand, we all have certain memories we'd rather forget. But no matter how hard we try, we can't erase certain specific experiences that conjure up awful feelings. They stick in our minds like glue. We simply can't forget them or get over them.

That's why some people are so unhappy today. They can't get past the *past*. If only they could press Ctrl-Alt-Del, they could re-boot, erasing the memories. But they can't.

The past has a way of haunting us, and many young people today have issues they wish they could get over. Sometimes years go by, and we think we've overcome them. Then the pain resurfaces.

It may encourage you to know that people in Scripture were no different. They were just people, with all kinds of baggage. Name a painful experience, and you'll likely find someone in Scripture who has it buried deep within them. Death, sin, sickness, family problems, lying, murder, adultery, abandonment, abuse, bitterness, and cruelty. Maybe it's not the *exact* issue you've faced, but you'll find almost identical sins and struggles right there in your own Bible.

DEVIL WITH A BLUE DRESS ON

Case in point: Mary Magdalene—a woman from the town of Magdala, hence her last name. Some have thought Mary was the prostitute Jesus forgave in Luke 7, but that was another woman. Surely it's not easy to overcome a life of prostitution, but Mary Magdalene's problem was even more severe—if you can believe that.

Mary was haunted by hell itself.

Specifically, Mary had *seven* demons living inside her! These foul devils had made a comfortable home in her. They were in charge, having taken over her body and mind. She was possessed.

What caused this to happen? Was she an idol worshipper? A Satanist? Was she involved with witchcraft? Who knows? In fact, the Bible never tells us what causes demonic possession. A widely accepted belief is that a demon must be *invited* into a person's life, or at least enter through some evil practice, such as the occult. For all we know, these powerful spirits may have simply stormed the gates of Mary's heart, overpowering her will, conquering her spirit, and taking over her body. They could have attacked her mind as terrorists do, kidnapping her heart and holding her will hostage. How could Mary have resisted the combined strength of seven demons? We don't know *how* it happened. We just know it *did*.

And if hers was similar to other possessions, she experienced some or all of the following:

- Mental Torture: Mass confusion. Deep, agonizing frustration. Perverse, wicked thoughts. An inability to think coherently.
- Social Excommunication: Separation from normal life, family, and society.
- Emotional Torment: Realistic, horrible fears. Nightmares even while awake.
- Physical Pain: Self-mutilation. Lingering scars, lasting reminders of satanic captivity.
- Volitional Slavery: Evil choices and a vile vocabulary. Being controlled by a force greater than yourself.

Perhaps Mary displayed these ghastly traits. If so, she was a wild, uncontrollable monster. This woman from Magdala was tortured in her soul and maybe even tormented others. Bottom line: Mary was completely controlled by a host of evil entities inhabiting her body. She was helpless while under the irresistible influence of those seven demons. Tormented within, she was hopeless case.

A lost cause.

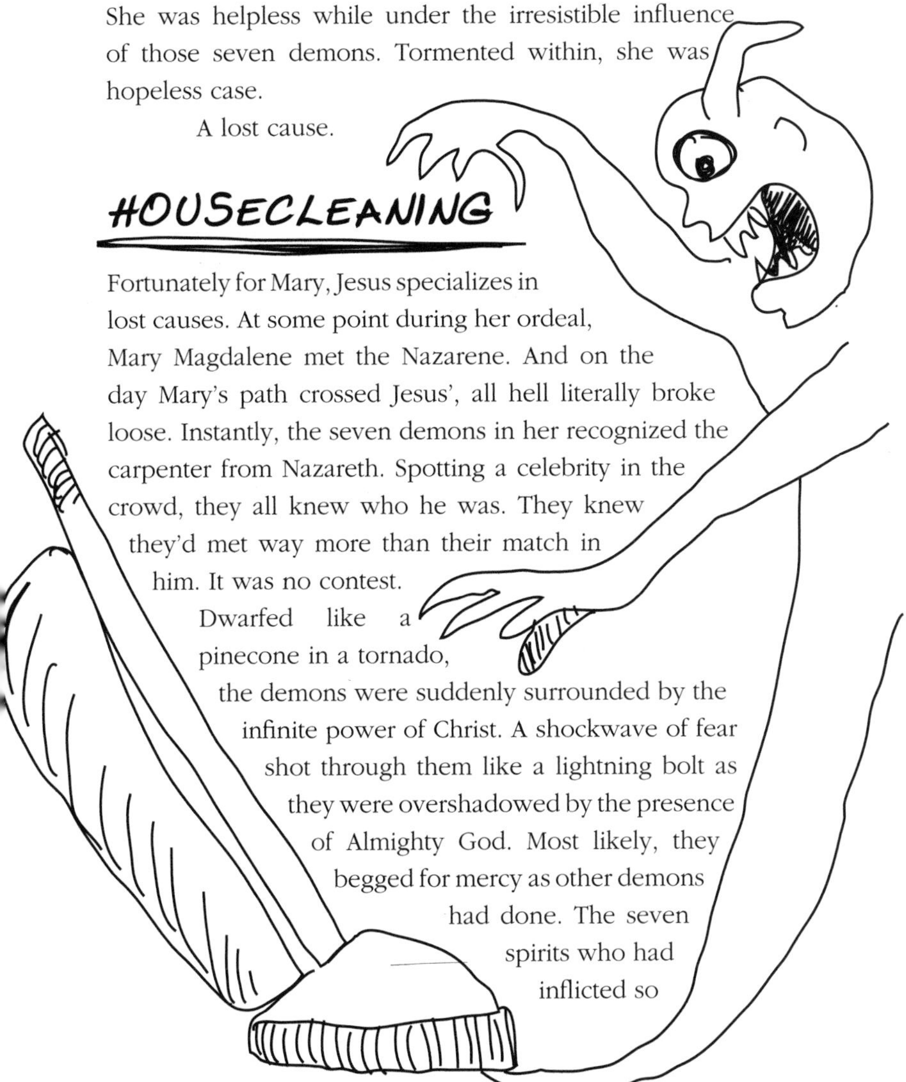

HOUSECLEANING

Fortunately for Mary, Jesus specializes in lost causes. At some point during her ordeal, Mary Magdalene met the Nazarene. And on the day Mary's path crossed Jesus', all hell literally broke loose. Instantly, the seven demons in her recognized the carpenter from Nazareth. Spotting a celebrity in the crowd, they all knew who he was. They knew they'd met way more than their match in him. It was no contest.

Dwarfed like a pinecone in a tornado, the demons were suddenly surrounded by the infinite power of Christ. A shockwave of fear shot through them like a lightning bolt as they were overshadowed by the presence of Almighty God. Most likely, they begged for mercy as other demons had done. The seven spirits who had inflicted so much fear and torment on others now found themselves full of dread and terror.

Though the Bible doesn't say, Jesus probably uttered a single word—*Go!*—and they exited Mary's body like rats jumping off a sinking ship. No lengthy exorcism here. No religious ritual. No incantations. Just a word from the Son of Man and they were gone.

The woman from Magdala was free.

Of course, they would've returned to Mary in full force unless a greater Power had not taken up residence in her heart (Matthew 12:43-45). Fortunately for Mary, her house was now under new management. She was filled once again, not with seven, but with One. A "No Vacancy" sign hung outside her heart. She was perfectly cured, completely delivered by Jesus. And for the first time in a long, long time, she was stable, sane, secure...and *saved*!

Can you see Mary looking up at Jesus, clearly exhausted from her ordeal, gazing into her Savior's smiling eyes with a cleansed, grateful heart? Her eyes welled up with tears as the reality of what had just happened began to sink in. She could hardly believe it. The monsters would never shout her name again. Her living nightmare was finally over...

Or was it?

HELL'S HURDLES

Several things might have happened at this point. Mary could have said a heartfelt "thank you" to Jesus and gone home to Magdala. And no one would've blamed her for this. Jesus healed many who, after receiving their miracle, simply went back home.

But something else could have happened. Even though Mary was delivered from her demons, the awful memory of her captivity could've haunted her like a recurring dream. Perhaps there were physical wounds or disfigurement of her body that served to remind her daily of her demonic ordeal. The demons were gone, but what had they left behind? Had they left Mary's mind trashed like a hotel room destroyed by partying rock stars? What permanent damage had they inflicted on her? And how would it affect her new life with Christ?

After all, let's be real. A difficult past is hard to overcome, no matter who you are. It can be a powerful magnet, pulling you irresistibly towards the darkness again.

Following Mary's deliverance, some former friends, family, and townspeople surely doubted they'd see any permanent change in "a person like her." She might "get religion" for a few months, but that would be it. She might be temporarily spellbound by the Galilean magician, but before long she'd wake up and snap out of it. She'd go back to her old self. It was only a matter of time.

The 12 disciples could have joined in this ministry of discouragement. They might have quenched her newfound passion for Christ. After all, rabbis didn't usually have women disciples, and the all-male group might have preferred to keep it a guys-only thing.

But let's believe the best and assume the disciples *did* welcome Mary into the fellowship with open arms. There's still one more reason she might have had enormous difficulty overcoming her past. True, Jesus had forgiven her, but would she be able to *enjoy* that forgiveness? Would her life really change? Or would she become paralyzed by feelings of guilt and unworthiness? Would her former life haunt her, pushing her over the edge into despair? Would Mary constantly wonder if she would get beyond her past and on to a new life? Would she forever be looking over her shoulder to see if the demons were coming back to get her? Would she ever make it as a disciple?

Haunting obstacles and huge hurdles like these may have greeted Mary as she took her first Christian baby steps. And any one of them could have prevented her from experiencing her new life with Jesus.

Think back over the past few years. How many of your friends have made a decision to follow Christ at a youth camp, conference, or retreat, only to sink right back into their old ways in a matter of weeks? How many didn't make it beyond their past, beyond the things that originally kept them from God?

And where are they now?

Failing to make a clean break with the past, allowing unhealthy influences to remain in your life, not making new friendships, falling back into old ways without first being grounded in the new Way—all these are reasons Jesus gives that people don't survive in the Christian life (Mark 4:1-20). We have to face the reality that it's not always going to be easy.

- It's not easy to break away from long-time friendships.
- It's not easy to conquer drug addiction.
- It's not easy to get past anger, hatred, and bitterness.
- It's not easy to get over your parents' divorce.
- It's not easy to overcome a difficult past.
- It's not easy to recover from rape.
- It's not easy to climb out of the pit of depression.
- It's not easy to ignore years of love deprivation and neglect.
- It's not easy to erase memories of sexual cruelty or child abuse.
- It's not easy to move past an abortion.
- It's not easy to break free from something that has controlled you for so long.

No, it's not easy. But it's possible when Jesus lives inside you.

MOVING ON

Fortunately for Mary, she had met the answer to her problem. She embraced a Savior who had earned a reputation for doing something no one else had done… giving women hope. Jesus raised women from second-class social status, giving them equality with men (Galatians

3:28). He treated them with dignity instead of humiliation. But beyond all these things, Jesus gave Mary forgiveness, deliverance, and salvation. She was now a friend of God (Romans 5:10).

So what *is* the rest of Mary's story? How did she respond to God's gift of grace and salvation? I'm happy to report that Mary became one of Jesus' most devoted and passionate followers. She also financially supported Jesus' ministry (Luke 8:2-3). She had much for which to be grateful, and she demonstrated her love through faithful devotion. When every disciple except John was cowering under the covers at home, Mary stood by her Savior while Roman soldiers brutally hammered him onto a cross (John 19:25). She cared enough to prepare his body for burial (Mark 16:1). She later brought materials to embalm him and was the first at the tomb after the resurrection (Mark 16:2).

God's reward for Mary's devotion was that she became the first to see the risen Redeemer (Mark 16:9). Her conversation with Jesus after his resurrection is a scene so tender it brings tears to your eyes (John 20:11-18).

There's no denying it—Mary came from a terrible past, one few of us will ever know. But she overcame it, leaving it all behind, moving on to a brand new life with Christ.

What can we learn from Mary? How can her story encourage us? Piecing together what we know about her from Scripture, here's what we observe about this remarkable woman.

First, Mary wanted to be wherever Jesus was. She stayed as close to Jesus as she possibly could. She didn't care if he was teaching on a hillside, lounging at someone's house, or even being crucified. She followed him wherever he went, no matter what the cost. She took advantage of every opportunity to deepen her relationship with Christ.

Second, Mary never looked back. Though powerless to erase the memory of her past, through Christ, she erased the *effect* that memory had on her. She broke the power of her past by focusing on her future. Like Mary, we too need to let go of anything that slows us down from running the race (Hebrews 12:2). Is anything or anyone keeping you from pursuing Jesus in your life? Is anything slowing you down, hindering your progress? If so, it's gotta go. Use God's power and drop it like a bad habit—*today.*

Third, Mary demonstrated her love for God. She invested her financial resources in his ministry. She was now *Jesus-possessed* and he had her heart, mind, soul, and body...even her bank account! Does he have all of you? I'm convinced Mary told her story to others wherever she went, sharing the love, hope, and power that come through a relationship with Jesus.

There are few things more exciting than seeing someone come to Christ from a "rough" past. They're like a family treasure snatched from a house fire. They are trophies of grace, stolen from Satan's private collection. These are lives worth celebrating every day.

Maybe you're thinking: *I don't have a difficult past. In fact, my life has been relatively smooth—no major traumas or past tragedies to overcome.* As a result, you may have a hard time relating to someone like Mary. So what does this woman have to teach you?

Well, she shows us that nobody is beyond the reach of Jesus. *Nobody.* So be careful not to dismiss anyone as hopeless. As long as there is breath, there is hope for anyone without Christ.

★ *Pray* for them.

Mary's story can also remind us how hard it can be to break free from a difficult past. This ought to give you compassion, understanding, and patience for others. Remember that we are all "in process" (Philippians 1:6).

★ *Be patient* with them.

Knowing that people such as Mary can change should motivate you to extend God's love to everyone. The Christ living inside you is the only hope for mankind. Share this hope.

Reach out to others.

Finally, Mary's complete commitment to Jesus makes her one of history's most devoted followers of Christ.

★ *Follow* her example.

Yes, Mary did get over her difficult past, but she never, ever got over Jesus.

Have you?

Are you haunted by your past? Are there experiences and issues you just can't seem to get over? You may find it comforting to know that the people in Scripture were no different. Name a painful experience, and you'll likely find someone in Scripture who has it buried deep within them. Death, sin, sickness, family problems, lying, murder, adultery, abandonment, abuse, bitterness, cruelty—whatever you've faced, you'll find someone with the same sins and struggles right there in your own Bible.

CHAPTER 7

MUSCLE-BOUND LUST-HOUND

HOW CAN I STOP MESSING UP MY LIFE?

SAMSON

One of the saddest statements in the whole Bible occurs in the last verse of Judges: "In those days Israel had no king, so the people did whatever seemed right in their own eyes" (Judges 21:25 NLT).

It was a time when people totally lived for themselves, not caring how their actions affected others. And this wasn't just true of pagan nations. It also applied to God's people. Here's the story:

Moses delivered Israel from Egypt (that whole "Red Sea" episode). After walking in circles for 40 years, Mo takes a dirt nap, and Israel's leadership passes to Joshua. General Joshua leads the nation into the land God had promised them. They experience some wins and losses during their first season conquering the land. But over time, Israel forgot how great God was and began acting just like the surrounding pagan nations. Obviously, the Lord wasn't too happy with this, so he disciplined Israel by allowing those other nations to conquer them. This got their attention, and they cried out to God, confessing their sin.

God responded by rescuing them through a *judge*, or deliverer (hence the book of "Judges"). These judges were usually skilled warriors and led Israel to victory in battle. But then, after a few years of serving the Lord, Israel would start worshipping pagan gods again, and the cycle would repeat itself. Idolatry. Captivity. Confession. Deliverance.

In fact, this cycle occurred seven times. And that's where we meet Samson, the last judge.

As you probably know, Samson possessed unbelievable physical strength. A massive physical specimen, he was the Incredible Hulk in sandals;

Schwarzenegger in a loincloth. Nobody could touch him. He could lift thousands of pounds and fight with phenomenal quickness. But his strength wasn't the result of countless hours spent in the weight room. His muscle came from heaven, a supernatural gift.

To understand Samson's story, we have to see the big picture of his life, beginning with his birth. Let's click through the DVD of his life story.

DESTINY'S CHILD

Scene 1: His Birth and Dedication (Judges 13)

Samson's parents were unable to have children. But in time, God's angel visited his mom, announcing the coming birth of a son. He instructed her to make the boy a Nazarite, meaning the boy would be set apart for God's service. This vow included total abstinence from alcohol, never touching anything dead, and never cutting your hair. (Samuel and John the Baptist would later take this same lifelong vow.) But the most important part of the angel's message was about Samson's mission, or life purpose, which was to "begin the deliverance of Israel from the hands of the Philistines" (13:5). This deliverance continued during Samuel's time and was completed during the reign of King David (when he killed Goliath).

Manoah (Samson's dad) asked the angel to visit them again to "teach us how to bring up the boy who is to be born" (13:8). He asked the angel's name, only to learn it is "beyond understanding" (13:18), a word translated "Wonderful" in Isaiah 9:6. Many Bible scholars believe this angel was the Son of God appearing in angelic form.

Apparently, so did Manoah and his wife, because they promptly worshipped him, declaring, "We have seen God!" (13:19-22).

Months later, Samson was born and began to grow. After a while, something began to stir within him (13:25). That "something" was a desire to fulfill his destiny, to become who he was made to be and accomplish his life purpose. But something else was stirring inside Samson's chiseled frame. Along with an undeniable desire to deliver his countrymen from oppression was a parallel urge to fulfill another, less honorable passion.

LIVING LIKE A ROCK STAR

Scene 2: Samson Marries a Philistine (Judges 14)

Passing through the portals of puberty, Samson experienced what all young men do at that age—a curiosity about the opposite sex. As you know, the teenage years are a time of change: physically, socially, and mentally. It's when guys begin caring about things they never cared about before, things like personal appearance, hair, deodorant, bathing—*good* things! Noticing girls for the first time, they even start *liking* them! You know what I'm talking about, don't you? (Psst...girls, here's a secret. Guys haven't changed in thousands of years. They're still basically *hormones in tennis shoes.*) Samson was no different, only he wore sandals.

Though this interest in the opposite sex is natural and God-given, Samson's desire for God soon took a back seat to his desire for women. Like a fire, this urge has to be contained or it quickly gets out of control. Unfortunately, Samson allowed a wildfire to rage inside him and became a man ruled by his emotions and hormones. He was a slave to his lustful desires much as Israel was to the Philistines.

One day Samson spotted a Philistine woman and told his parents to "get her for me as my wife" (14:2). Manoah and his wife objected to their son's request on two grounds:

1) It was against God's law to marry non-Jews. (Exodus 34:15-17; Deuteronomy 7:1-4)

2) The Philistines were Israel's arch-enemies.

Few things break a parent's heart more than to see a son or daughter make unhealthy choices, especially when it comes to relationships and romance. But though this marriage was against God's law, the Lord would nevertheless use it to accomplish his purpose through Samson (Judges 14:4). Remember, God can turn a failure into victory.

On the way to meet his soon-to-be bride, Samson encountered a lion and tore it apart with his bare hands (14:6). When he finally met the woman, Samson really liked what he saw. Now, it's perfectly normal to like your fiancée, right? But this is where we see Samson's fatal flaw, the crack in the strong man's character. He focused totally on this woman's outward features. Samson's sensuality was too strong. Again, these desires are a normal part of growing up, but they can easily turn sinful if not placed under God's control.

You may remember back in 2003, when Las Vegas illusionist Roy Horn was horribly mauled and mutilated when his 800-pound white tiger turned on him. Like a bolt of lightning, the beast pounced on Roy during a routine he had performed hundreds of times before. Clamping its powerful jaws down on Roy's neck, the mighty cat dragged Roy around the stage like a limp piece of meat before finally releasing him. Roy Horn rediscovered the hard way that tigers will always be wild animals at heart. It's their nature. In a heartbeat, they can turn on you, and that's why they must be controlled at all times.

You might say Samson had a "tiger in his tank." His sexual passions repeatedly turned on him, bringing a load of pain and heartache. And speaking of big cats, on the way back home, Samson saw the dead carcass of that lion he had killed, filled now with honeybees. He stooped to sample the honey, violating his Nazarite vow (14:8-9). Later, Samson enjoyed a seven-day wedding feast where he likely drank wine, violating his vow a second time (14:10).

At that party, he presented his 30 groomsmen with a customary riddle. Samson promised them all a new set of clothes if they solved it. After seven days of partying, Samson grew weak in his fiancée's arms, and

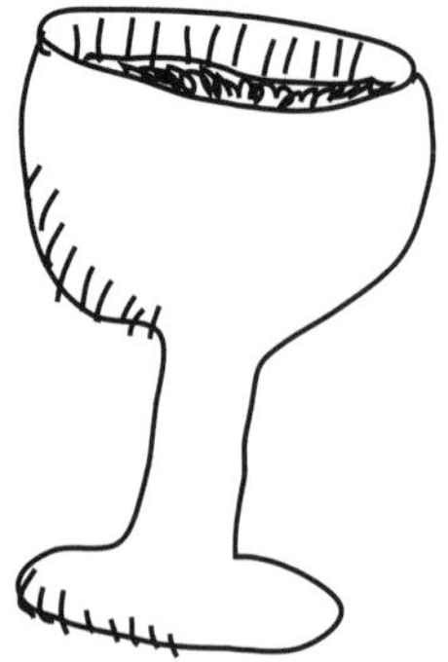

she enticed the riddle's answer out of him. She told the groomsmen, which caused Samson to explode with anger (another untamed "cat out of the bag"). In retaliation, he traveled 23 miles to the Philistine town of Ashkelon, killed 30 men, and delivered their clothing to his groomsmen. After pouting a while at home, he returned to claim his bride, only to discover his father-in-law had given her away to his best man! (14:20-15:1) He offered Samson a younger sister instead.

Wrong answer.

We see Samson again explode with rage, catch 300 foxes, fasten their tails together, tie a torch to their tails, and set them loose into the Philistines' fields of grain. In response, the Philistines take his wife and her father and burn them! (Nice people, huh?) Samson's revengeful spirit came back to bite him like a scorpion. But though he's reaping the bitter fruit of a lustful heart, he's *still* not learning the lesson.

OPENING UP A "CAN OF WHOOP"

Scene 3: Samson Slaughters the Philistines (15:8-20)

Pick up the newspaper. Revenge is still very much in vogue. A Palestinian bombs an Israeli bus. In response, an Israeli shoots a Palestinian leader. In U.S. cities, the murder of a teenage boy is met by a drive-by shooting on the other side of town two days later. All over the globe, the never-ending cycle of vengeance and violence is repeated.

Things were no different in Samson's time. To get revenge for the murder of his fiancée, Samson slaughtered a few hundred Philistines. (Think of a battle scene from *Braveheart*. It's not a pleasant sight. War and the taking of human life never are.) Then he retreated under a rock, sulking while the Philistines looked for him (15:8-9). Meanwhile, 3,000 fellow Israelites tried to persuade him to give himself up, which he eventually did. But though Israel was content to be ruled by the Philistines, Samson wasn't. He had other plans.

Bound with new ropes, Samson was led back to Lehi. Suddenly they rushed at him, shouting a battle cry. God's Spirit came mightily upon Samson, and he took the jawbone of a freshly killed donkey and killed 1,000 Philistines! A *thousand*! Later, they named the place "Jawbone Hill" (15:17). Can you believe all this?!

Samson was understandably thirsty after this battle. God provided water from a spring (15:18-19). But the pendulum of Samson's mood was about to swing once again in the other direction, from anger and vengeance back to lust.

SLEEPING WITH THE ENEMY

Scene 4: Samson Meets His Match (16:1-3)

Samson's pursuit of God ran hot and cold—with no in-between. He was a man of extremes, his unusual physical strength equaled only by his moral weakness. Like fire, sexual desire can quickly burn us (Proverbs 6:26-28). And we're talking third-degree burns, leaving long-lasting scars.

Some time after his victory over the Philistines, possibly near the end of his life, Samson went down to Gaza. We don't know why. But while there, he spotted a prostitute and spent the night with her. (Man, is he off-course with his life purpose or what!) A rumor spread that mighty Samson was in town, so the Philistines surrounded the house, planning a raid on him at daybreak. Samson woke up in the middle of the night, ripped the city gates off their hinges, and carried them to the top of the hill for everyone to see. Now Gaza was defenseless. Picture this scene! Rippling muscles tearing wood and iron like Silly Putty. This dude is buff! And though Samson shouldn't have been there, amazingly God used even this circumstance to accomplish his purposes.

HAIR TODAY, GONE TOMORROW

Scene 5: Samson is Captured by the Philistines (16:4-21)

Samson was then between 35 and 40 years old. He met another pagan woman and fell in love with her. (Imagine that!) Apparently, sexual immorality isn't something you outgrow with age. It's not just a "teenage stage" or a "college thing." Samson changed sex partners like some people change shoes. Never satisfied, his heartaches were a direct result of following *his* passions, not *God's.* And he was on course for another head-on collision with a major disappointment.

This heartache's name was Delilah. Her name means *desire* or *flirt,* and she certainly lived up to her name. Infatuated with emotion and lust, Samson convinced himself she was *the one.* Or perhaps he figured Delilah would be just one more trophy in his collection of female conquests.

On the contrary, it was Samson who got conquered this time. After being offered 1,100 pieces of silver (around $3,000), Delilah, flirting and using every trick in the book, enticed Samson to reveal the source of his strength. A symbol of his vow to God, Samson's hair was the secret of his enormous power (16:5-19).

Samson's life purpose and dedication to God meant so little to him at this point that he was willing to sell the secret of his supernatural strength for a kiss. Sensuality clouded his ability to think clearly. Like a narcotic, it dulled his senses. However, Samson's trouble wasn't so much a broken vow as one that had never been taken seriously.

With honey on her lips and poison in her heart, Delilah was paid for her diabolical work (16:18). They shaved Samson's head. And his strength left him.

Delilah played a relatively minor role in Samson's life, but her effect was devastating. It's like the girl who becomes pregnant after just one sexual experience. It's like getting a damaged reputation after only a few dates. It wasn't the *length* of the relationship but rather the *nature* of it that sunk Samson.

And he never fully recovered.

Friend, beware of *Delilahs*—male and female—who sow seeds of immorality, unbelief, and deceit in you. Guard your heart from these people.

"Delilahs" can also be *ideas, priorities,* and *values*—and they can be found in books, movies, and magazines, on the Internet, and even in your own heart. How can you recognize them? By evaluating them against the standard of God's Word. Then, with God's help, move on. I've known Christian teenagers who realize it's their non-Christian boyfriends or girlfriends who need to be dropped like a bad habit. They made that hard choice—never looking back and raising their standards of whom they would and would not date.

Unfortunately, Samson was not a man with high moral standards. He was not a man of the *Book* (Psalm 119:11). How ironic that the strongest man in the world wasn't brought down by gladiators or armies, but rather by one petite, pretty girl. What ropes and cords couldn't do, a little sensuality did. Samson's commitment to God meant nothing as he gladly surrendered his secret to a Philistine babe.

One of Samson's big problems was in not recognizing his weakness. He was blind to it, and like the Greek hero Achilles (the one with the weak heel), his unprotected area proved to be his downfall. A weakness is often a blind spot, and we need others to point it out to us. Everyone else could see Samson's weakness (the Philistines, his parents, Delilah, and *every woman he met).* Friends point out weaknesses. Enemies take advantage of them (Proverbs 27:6). What is your "Achilles heel"?

Tragically, after his haircut, Samson didn't even know the Lord had left him (16:20).

And then they captured him.

BRINGING THE HOUSE DOWN

Final Scene: Samson's Last Performance (16:22-31)

The Philistines, not known for their kindness to their enemies, gouged out Samson's eyes (16:21), literally drilling his eyeballs out. Ouch! Then they brought him to Gaza, bound him with chains, and threw him in prison. Remember, it was in Gaza where he uprooted the city gates (16:3).

During the day he ground meal between millstones with a harness around his neck. It was backbreaking work normally reserved for donkeys.

But during his slavery experience Samson's hair began growing back. And as his hair returned, so did his reason. He turned his heart back to the Lord—back to God's purpose for his life.

One night, more than 3,000 Philistines (with their rulers) gathered to offer great sacrifice to Dagon, their god of harvest and grain (16:23-24). Many temples were built to this fictitious deity, whose worship included human sacrifice. But these temples also doubled as local entertainment centers (similar to a concert hall or auditorium), where thousands gathered to see the torture and humiliation of prisoners. They were massive structures supported by two huge wooden pillars mounted on stone bases, with a roof large enough to hold thousands of people!

That night the feature act was Samson, entertaining them with his strength. This citywide Philistine festival celebrated Samson's deliverance into their hands (16:23). It was a circus, with Samson in the center ring. Everyone was drunk and having a great time mocking the once mighty Samson, now blind and led around by a servant boy (16:26). What a pitiful sight! Mighty Samson—dependent on a little boy. The last thing on Samson's mind that night was beautiful women or sex.

Amid the shouts, jeers, and laughter of the massive crowd, Samson whispered a desperate prayer, "O Sovereign God, remember me. O God, please strengthen me once more" (16:28). It's as if he were saying, *God, I know I've blown it. I confess I have ignored my calling and commitment. But before I die, let me return to you and fulfill my destiny.*

With help from the boy, Samson maneuvered himself between the two massive pillars, placed his faith in God, and pushed with all his might (16:30). The huge temple creaked, cracked, and crumbled, caving in and killing thousands, including Samson.

Weighed down by past guilt, and in spite of his sin, Samson was still used by God to accomplish his purpose.

SO WHAT?

Though marked by frequent failure, Samson still finished strong, ending up in God's "Hall of Faith" (See Hebrews 11:32-33). So, what can you learn from Samson?

1. It's sad to be remembered for what you *might have been*. Not living up to your potential is tragic, because you can't turn back time. You get only one shot in life. Don't waste it.

2. In spite of failure and weakness, God can still use you to accomplish his purpose for your life.

3. One area of weakness can overshadow many areas of strength. This is the great tragedy of Samson's life. What would you say is one of your weakest areas?

4. Sexual sins often have visible and lasting consequences including guilt, pregnancy, emotional scars, and irreparable damage to relationships. Samson's sexual scars were like needle tracks in a heroin addict's arms. What are you doing to protect yourself from falling into sexual sin?

5. It's never too late to start over. You can still accept God's grace and experience his forgiveness, turning your defeats into victory. Like Samson and the thief on the cross, you too can pray, *O Lord, remember me...* If you've lost your way, forgotten God, or fallen into sin, know that God has not forgotten you.

No matter what has happened in the past or what you've done, you can still turn your heart toward heaven today and get back in the race.

It's never too late to start over. You can still accept God's grace and experience his forgiveness, turning your defeats into victory. With Samson and the thief on the cross, you too can pray, "O Lord, remember me..." If you've lost your way, forgotten God, or fallen into sin, know that God has not forgotten you.

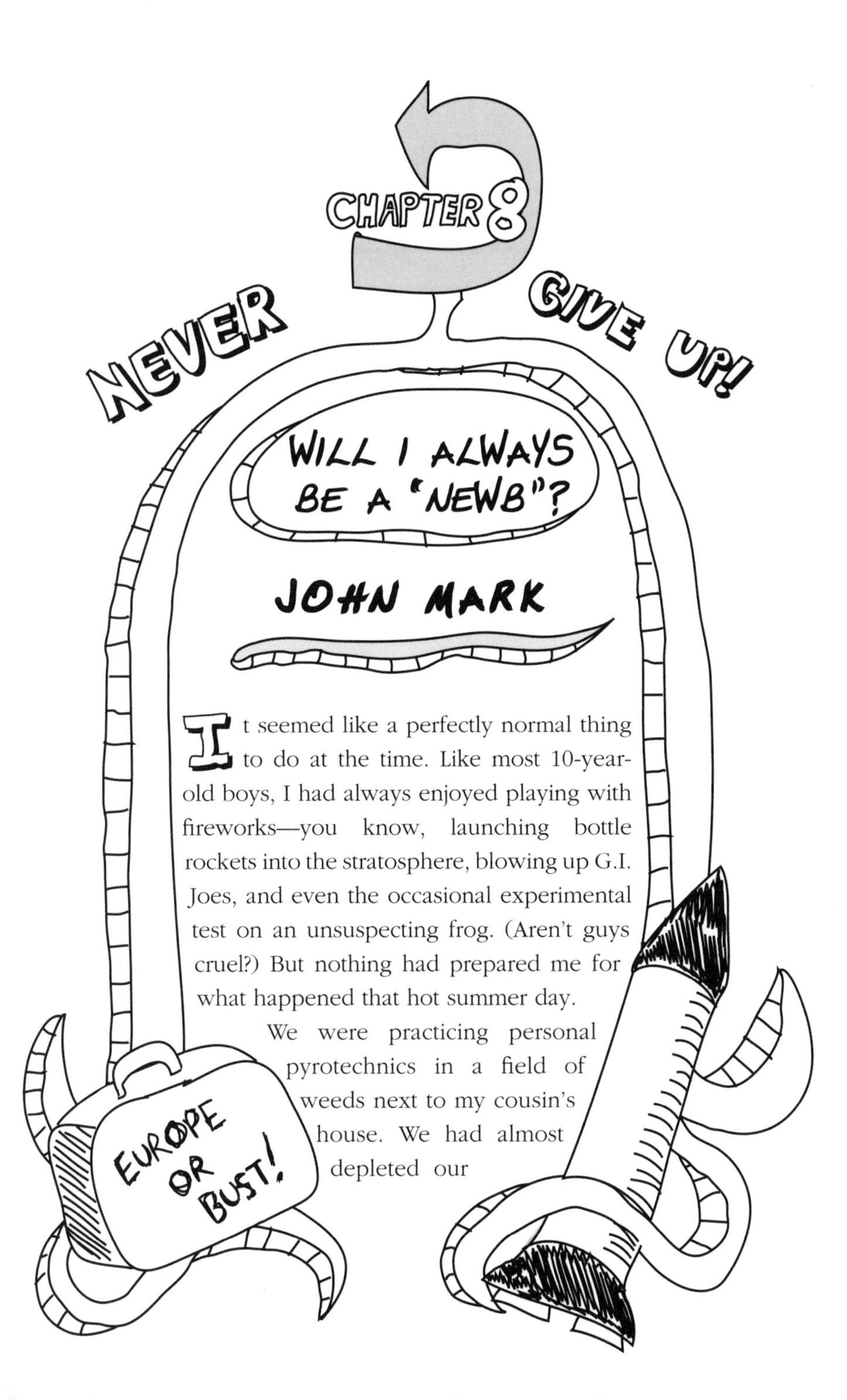

WILL I ALWAYS BE A "NEWB"?

JOHN MARK

It seemed like a perfectly normal thing to do at the time. Like most 10-year-old boys, I had always enjoyed playing with fireworks—you know, launching bottle rockets into the stratosphere, blowing up G.I. Joes, and even the occasional experimental test on an unsuspecting frog. (Aren't guys cruel?) But nothing had prepared me for what happened that hot summer day.

We were practicing personal pyrotechnics in a field of weeds next to my cousin's house. We had almost depleted our storehouse of firecrackers when I smelled a strange odor. Turning in the direction of the scent, my eyes spotted something you never want to see in an open field—smoke!

It wasn't really *that much* smoke, just enough to cause us to dash over and check it out. Arriving at the source, we discovered a very small fire—no big deal, really. Quickly, we began stomping it out. But for some strange reason, it wasn't going out. In fact, the fire was spreading…rapidly! In spite of our desperate dance on the flames, it soon became clear we were losing the battle of the blaze. So, we did what came naturally.

We ran.

Oddly, it never occurred to us to call for help. Apparently (thankfully) it occurred to someone, because we soon heard the whir of a fire-truck siren. By that time half the field was engulfed in flames. Yeah, I know what you're thinking. We should have immediately called 9-1-1. Most people would have. But they didn't have 9-1-1 back then (though we did have phones!). Besides, we really thought the fire might die out eventually.

We were wrong.

Chalk one up to acting like kids. Let's just say our problem-solving skills were still "under construction." As a result, we failed to respond in a grown-up way. Some would call that immaturity, and they'd be right. I'm happy to report, however, that I have learned a lot over the years, and I'm much more mature now...at least I know when to call the fire department!

If all you knew about me was that I almost caught the world on fire once, you might think I was a total loser. But there's more to my story—much more. And the same is true for you. I bet you've done a few really unintelligent things in your life. You know, dumb decisions from the *"What was I thinking?"* file. Like the time you sneaked out of the house, only to be met at the front door by your mom and dad when you returned at 4 a.m. Or the time you answered your mom when she yelled, "*What do you think I am...stupid?"*

That's immaturity (with a little stupidity thrown in).

Well, it should comfort you to know the Bible is filled with stories of people who acted immaturely at some time in their lives. If all we knew about them was just that one incident, we would conclude they were big-time failures...*losers*. And that's why we need the rest of the story.

I WAS A TEENAGE DISCIPLE

Meet John Mark, as in the *Gospel of Mark*. Though we know virtually nothing about his childhood, we suspect

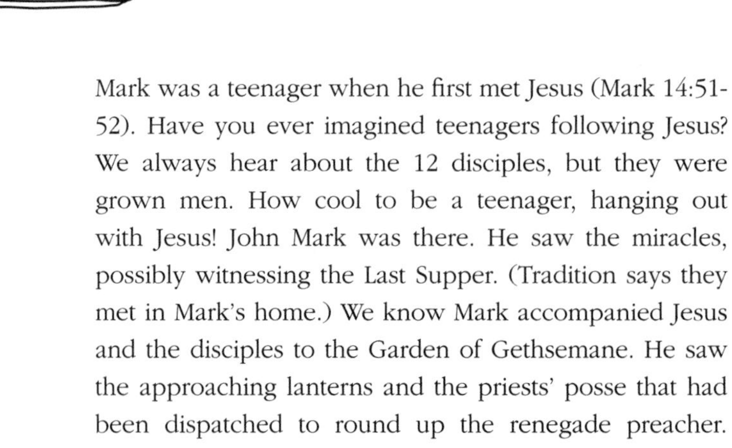

Mark was a teenager when he first met Jesus (Mark 14:51-52). Have you ever imagined teenagers following Jesus? We always hear about the 12 disciples, but they were grown men. How cool to be a teenager, hanging out with Jesus! John Mark was there. He saw the miracles, possibly witnessing the Last Supper. (Tradition says they met in Mark's home.) We know Mark accompanied Jesus and the disciples to the Garden of Gethsemane. He saw the approaching lanterns and the priests' posse that had been dispatched to round up the renegade preacher. That's when things got ugly. Perhaps peeking around an olive tree, Mark watched as a fight broke out, a fight that ended with Peter slashing off somebody's ear. During that incident, Mark himself was briefly captured by Roman soldiers but managed to slip out of his garment, running away into the night…*totally naked*!

I bet he had fun explaining his appearance to his mom when he got home.

"ME? A MISSIONARY?"

Other than this episode, we know little about John Mark—though it's believed that he became a charter member of the Jerusalem Church. (His house was a sort of "hub" for Christian activity in that city.) Many years later, the church gathered there for prayer while Peter was in prison (Acts 12:5).

Years passed. Mark was about 30 years old when his cousin Barnabas introduced him to his friend Paul. Barnabas and Paul were leaving for a missions trip, and Barnabas invited his cousin John Mark to go. This pioneer missionary journey must have seemed like the adventure of a lifetime to Mark, serving Paul and Barnabas as their ministry intern (Acts 13:5).

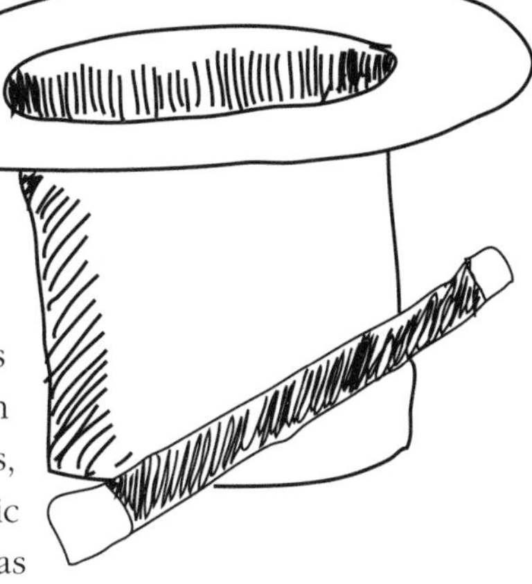

However, something happened on that trip. In short, Mark "choked," abandoning Paul and Barnabas and returning home. The real question is "Why?" What caused him to turn back? Scripture tells us they had a minor confrontation with a magician on the island of Cyprus, but aside from that, nothing traumatic or life threatening occurred. It was nothing compared with what would happen to Paul and Barnabas at Iconium, where they were almost murdered by an angry mob. It was nothing compared with what later happened in Lystra. There, some Jews motivated by religious hate stoned Paul, dragging him out of the city and leaving him for dead (14:19).

But John Mark was already home by that time and missed all this persecution. So what was his problem? Why did he abandon the men and the mission? Was he seasick—or just homesick? Did he question his purpose on the team? Did he not have what it took to be a missionary? Did he not count the cost before signing up? Did the confrontation with the magician trigger a fear-filled flashback to that awful night in the Garden of Gethsemane? It wasn't as if this were his first missions trip, either—he had previously accompanied Barnabas and Paul on a famine relief missions trip to Judea (Acts 12:25). So what was his deal?

Nobody knows, really. Whatever the reason, John Mark concluded early on he'd had enough…so he quit. Chalk one up to immaturity.

REPORT CARD
F
F
F

What about you? Ever felt like giving up on following God?

Keep in mind that Mark wasn't a teenager anymore. He was thirty-something when he flunked out of "missionary school." So how can we call his failure an *immature* decision?

Well, to begin with, immaturity isn't just something for teenagers. It's not an *age* thing. It's a *personal growth* thing. For example, when your dad suddenly starts disco dancing in the living room, you naturally race to shut the curtains for fear anyone might see the embarrassing spectacle, right? That may not be immaturity on his part. It may just be his way of…shall we say…*remembering*. (By the way, be nice to your parents. They're endowed with the unusual ability to embarrass you at will. So be good to them. Clean your room. Bribe them if you have to. Just don't do anything that might cause them to break down and "bust a rhyme" in front of your friends.)

We communicating?

So Dad's dance fever isn't the "juvenile behavior" we're talking about here. Instead, think of how totally weird it would be if your dad suddenly began sucking his thumb. *(Uh...Dad. What are you doing?)* Or how bizarre it'd be if your school principal refused to come out from under the covers, crying: "Nobody likes me at that school!

I'm not going back!" Or how baffling it is when church members fight about the color of the sanctuary carpet or whether to include drums in worship. *That's* immaturity.

Come to think of it, a lot of adults are immature. That's because maturity doesn't automatically come with age. It's something you have to work at. And sometimes difficult circumstances can force your immature areas to the surface. I think that's what happened with Mark. Though he was already an adult and no doubt progressing in his relationship with God, he (like us) still had some growing to do.

Ministry requires some maturity. It takes a certain amount of maturity to explain to a 17-year-old drug addict why Jesus is better for him than cocaine. It takes some maturity to show someone why yours is the only true God. Being 5,000 miles from home, across the ocean, or in another country standing on your own faith is a far cry from cleaning up a vacant lot in the name of Christ. Not to say there isn't value in that, but Paul and Barnabas' mission was to take the Good News about the Messiah to people who'd never heard it before—and who were very likely to be skeptical and hostile to the message.

Maybe…just maybe, Mark sensed that. Every hour he sailed across the Mediterranean took him farther away from the safety and security of home. This pioneer missionary stuff wasn't very glamorous, either. There were no five-star hotels. No gourmet meals. No Green Room before your gig. No other Christians waiting to welcome them or to provide lodging. No printed brochure highlighting where the good shopping would be. No luxury cabins on their cruise across the sea. No guarantees concerning what waited for them once they arrived.

Their missions trip would be a high-risk adventure, a flirt with danger and perhaps even death. Oh, and one more thing—it would be a lot of hard work. Early mornings, long days, and late nights. This evangelism excursion would be a huge leap—make that a *skydive*—of faith. And John Mark had forgotten to pack a parachute.

THE COMEBACK COUSIN

Several years ago I took a gamble by taking one of my students with me on a missions trip to England. To be honest, I wondered if he'd last the whole trip. I just wasn't convinced he was ready for the experience. However, I figured even if he didn't do much ministry, he could at least help with the sound equipment and luggage. To my surprise, he turned out to be the only person on our team who led anyone to Christ! Today he is pastor of missions in a church! Ironically, it was *I*, not he, who lacked faith. On the other hand, there have been times when I wished I *had* sent students home because they simply weren't mature enough to handle the experience.

I think that's where Paul and Barnabas found themselves after they returned. Each of them had different feelings about John Mark's decision to leave the work and go home. Later, as Paul was preparing for his second missionary journey, Barnabas suggested they take John Mark with them. Paul responded, "Are you out of your mind? He barely lasted a few weeks last time. We can't afford to take another risk on him. In fact, we won't. There's too much at stake here."

Well, maybe he didn't actually say those exact words, but that's what he felt. And so they debated...okay, they actually argued about it. (Yes, even mature people

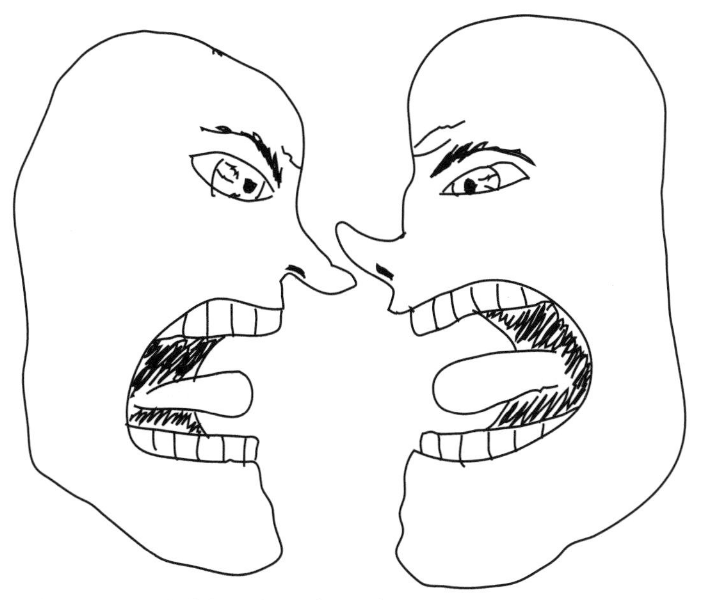

disagree and debate.) In fact, their "sharp disagreement" became so animated that they split up, dissolving their ministry partnership. Each man believed he was right and the other was wrong in the matter.

Paul took Silas on his second evangelistic expedition, while Barnabas invited John Mark to sail away to Cyprus with him (Acts 15:36-40). Now, that must have been a tough season of life for John Mark. Think about it. He had failed at being a missionary. And if he had formerly idolized the apostle Paul, wanting to be like him, he had obviously missed the mark. Further, Paul now thought he was a total loser. And when the greatest Christian who ever lived thinks you're a loser, that's a major bummer. Surely others also looked down on him, too—as Paul's opinion and recommendation as an apostle carried a lot of weight with the church.

John Mark just didn't have what it took…or so people thought.

But that's where cousin Barnabas stepped in. Taking him under his wing, Barnabas began the slow process of rebuilding John Mark's self-esteem and faith. Barnabas took him to Cyprus, probably to visit the church planted on their first trip there. It wasn't a long trip, not quite the "major leagues" of missions. But that may have been just what John Mark needed—a chance to prove himself at this level before attempting something greater for God. He needed time to grow into the ministry.

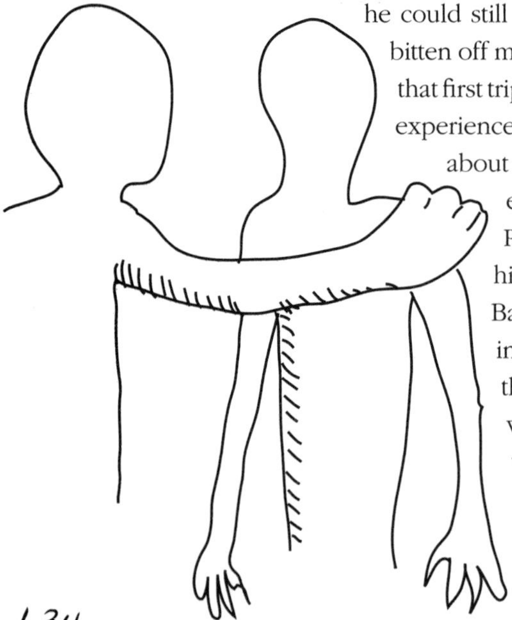

That trip with Barnabas proved to John Mark that he could still serve God. Maybe he had bitten off more than he could chew on that first trip with Paul. But through the experience he had learned something about ministry, missions, and especially himself. Though Paul was quick to exclude him from the next journey, Barnabas saw potential in his younger cousin, though I think Barnabas was motivated by more than just family loyalty. I believe it had something to do with who Barnabas was. His name actually means "son of encouragement," and he certainly lived up to that name. People who are encouragers see more than others see. They have the ability to see potential in others. They possess the gift that recognizes hidden promise in those written off by others.

Many times over the years students have said to me: "When nobody else gave me a chance or believed in me, you did."

It's one of the greatest compliments I'll ever receive.

That's exactly what Barnabas did for John Mark. He believed in him and gave him a second chance. He saw greatness lying dormant within John Mark. Ironically, Barnabas had done the same thing for Paul years earlier when nobody had believed in him (Acts 9:26-27).

It was during this time of rebuilding that Mark started hanging out with another fellow flunky, someone who had also experienced some major failure. His name was Peter, and we don't even have to talk about how he struck out in the big game. Remember how Peter denied Christ three times, swearing he didn't know him? Peter and Mark developed a close friendship, with Peter even referring to Mark as "my son" (1 Peter 5:13). Who better to mentor Mark than someone who had dealt with failure himself? Soon Peter described to Mark with picture-perfect detail the life and ministry of Jesus. This proved to be a divinely inspired friendship, as Mark, combining his own recollections with Peter's, became the very first person to write a New Testament book. Who would've thought it?

Talk about a second chance!

BACK IN BUSINESS

Fast-forward another 14 years. We haven't heard anything from John Mark, and Scripture says nothing about him. Then suddenly he resurfaces in the most unlikely place—a prison cell. That's surprising enough, but even more so when we discover he's there visiting an old friend: *Paul*!

The Apostle puts it this way: *"My fellow prisoner Aristarchus sends you his greetings, as does Mark, the cousin of Barnabas. (You have received instructions about him; if he comes to you, welcome him.)"* (Colossians 4:10)

Mark was in his fifties then. That's a long way from running naked in the Garden of Gethsemane. It was also 20 years past bailing out of a missions trip. That's history. Mark had done a lot of growing since then. He had matured in so many areas. And so had Paul. In fact, Mark would visit Paul many times during the apostle's last days in that Roman prison cell. Paul even grew to miss John Mark when he wasn't there with him and specifically asked for him on at least one occasion (2 Timothy 4:11). He could have asked for anyone, but he chose Mark.

I think Mark found himself in that prison because Paul had experienced a change of heart. Paul saw what happened when Barnabas took Mark in, becoming a life coach for him. He saw what happened when Peter came alongside Mark. The two shared a common failure and struggle. They also shared a mutual love for Jesus and a belief that failure is never final. Paul observed the value of a second chance and the importance of not dismissing people because of their immaturity. Paul also probably reflected on the time in his life when Barnabas had gone to bat for him.

I believe John Mark was in that prison cell because he had grown a lot over the years. Following his initial disappointment on that missions trip, Mark no doubt went through an incredible period of personal uncertainty. Barnabas and Peter treated him with grace, and he was able to extend that same grace to Paul as well. After all, you can't give away what you don't possess. As time passed, Mark grew in personal maturity. Maybe he even surprised himself by how much he grew. When word came that Paul was requesting his presence in faraway Rome, Mark couldn't pack his suitcase fast enough.

The journey from spiritual immaturity to maturity is a long one. It's a lifetime journey that takes you from ignorance to insight, from cowardice to confidence, from recklessness to responsibility.

We all have our own setbacks and stumbling blocks on our personal road to maturity. That's okay. Every season of life is a learning experience. So get up, shake it off, and keep moving. You'll never achieve perfection this side of heaven, but wherever you are, just remember this: John Mark never gave up.

And neither should you.

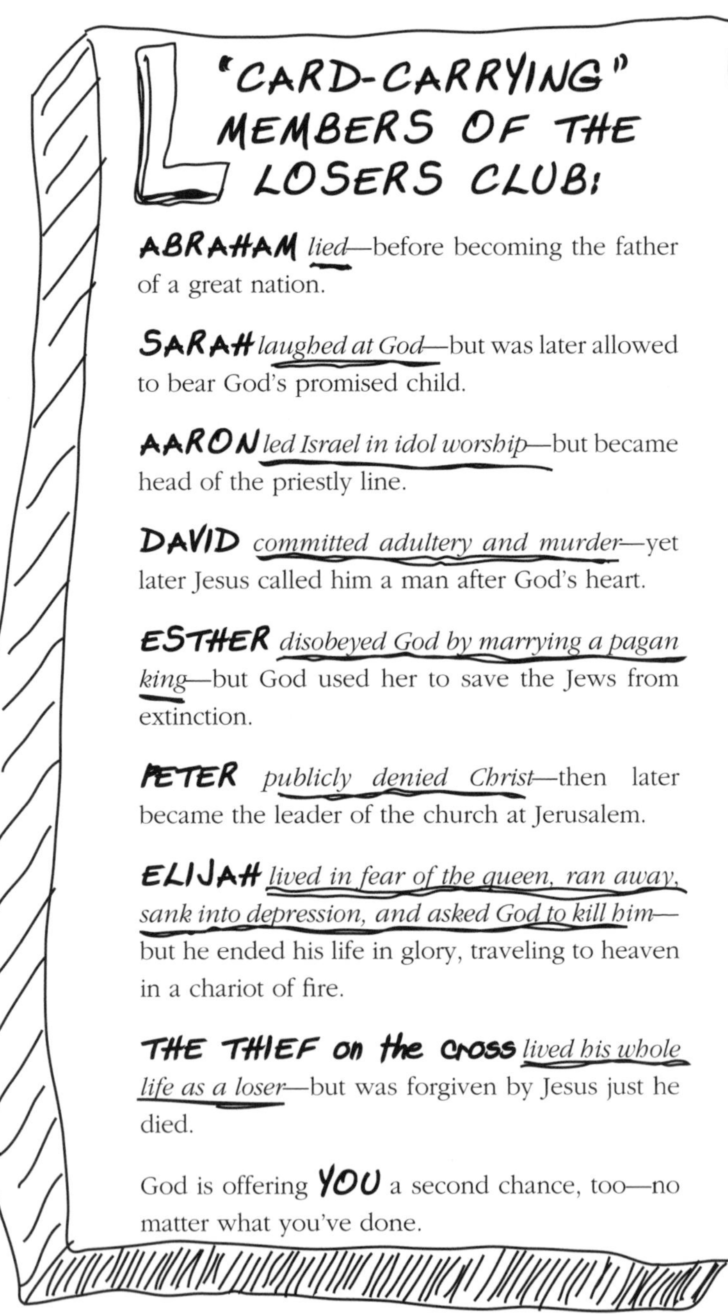

"CARD-CARRYING" MEMBERS OF THE LOSERS CLUB:

ABRAHAM *lied*—before becoming the father of a great nation.

SARAH *laughed at God*—but was later allowed to bear God's promised child.

AARON *led Israel in idol worship*—but became head of the priestly line.

DAVID *committed adultery and murder*—yet later Jesus called him a man after God's heart.

ESTHER *disobeyed God by marrying a pagan king*—but God used her to save the Jews from extinction.

PETER *publicly denied Christ*—then later became the leader of the church at Jerusalem.

ELIJAH *lived in fear of the queen, ran away, sank into depression, and asked God to kill him*—but he ended his life in glory, traveling to heaven in a chariot of fire.

THE THIEF on the cross *lived his whole life as a loser*—but was forgiven by Jesus just he died.

God is offering **YOU** a second chance, too—no matter what you've done.

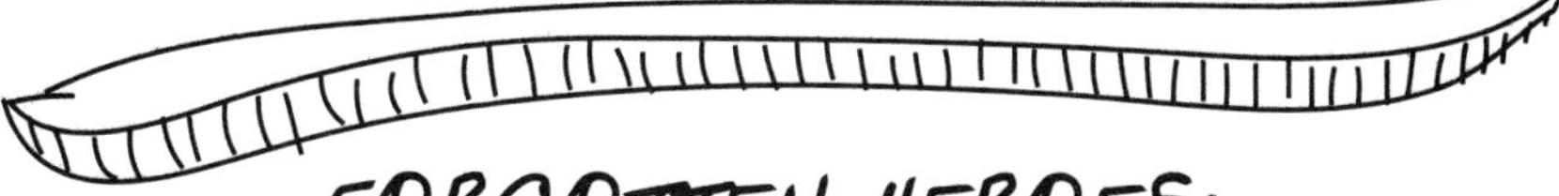

FORGOTTEN HEROES:

INSPIRATION FROM SCRIPTURE'S UNKNOWNS

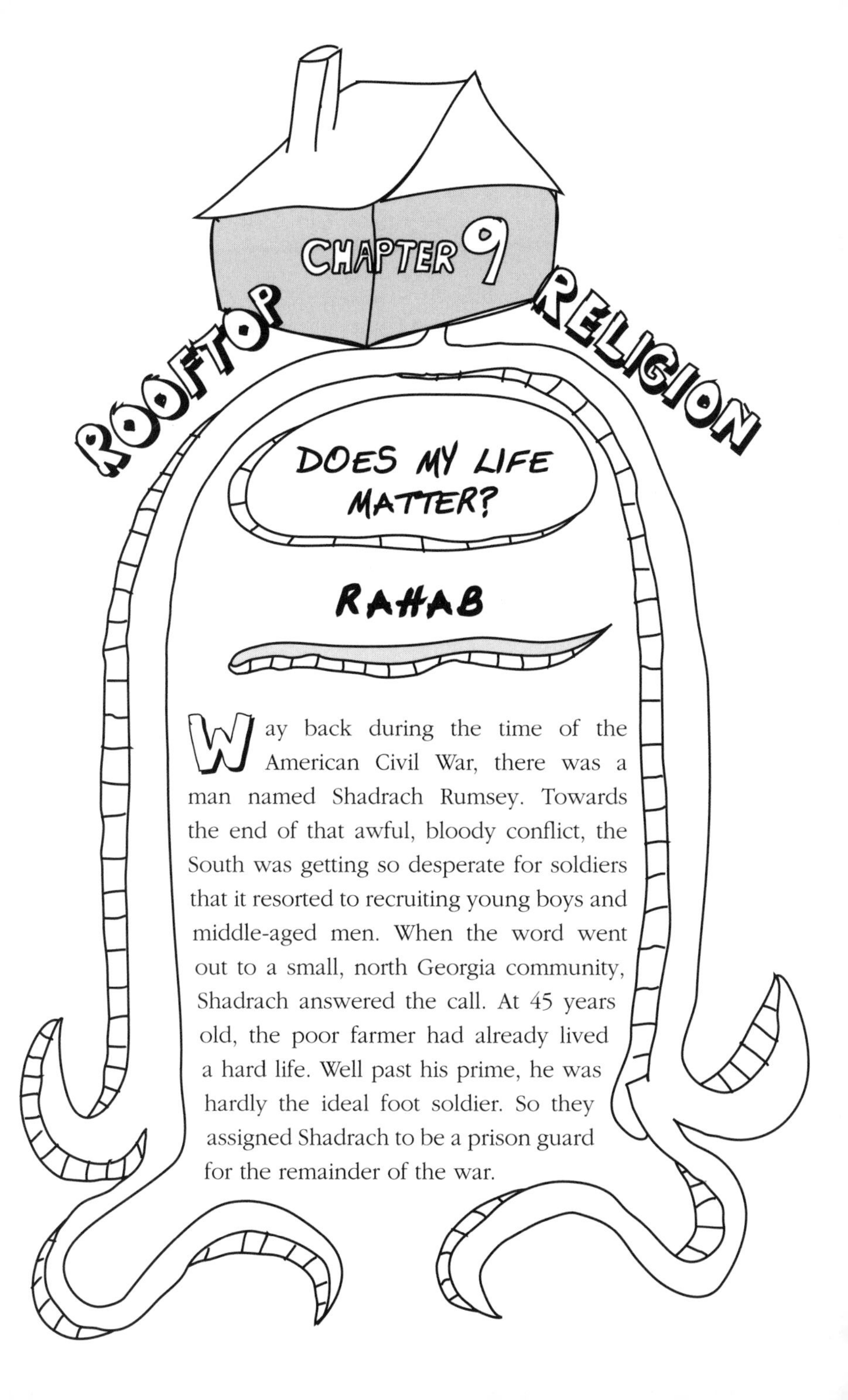

CHAPTER 9 ROOFTOP RELIGION

DOES MY LIFE MATTER?

RAHAB

Way back during the time of the American Civil War, there was a man named Shadrach Rumsey. Towards the end of that awful, bloody conflict, the South was getting so desperate for soldiers that it resorted to recruiting young boys and middle-aged men. When the word went out to a small, north Georgia community, Shadrach answered the call. At 45 years old, the poor farmer had already lived a hard life. Well past his prime, he was hardly the ideal foot soldier. So they assigned Shadrach to be a prison guard for the remainder of the war.

Some 35 years later, at age 80, Shadrach applied for a government pension for old soldiers as a last-ditch effort to secure income for his family. By this time, he was living with relatives, still trying to scratch out a living as a farmer. After filling out the application, there was a space at the bottom of the page reserved for the signature of the applicant. There, on that line, Shadrach took a fountain pen and carved out a big "X." Beside this were added the words *his mark*, meaning this was his signature.

The truth was that old Shadrach couldn't spell, write, or read. He wasn't much more than an illiterate hillbilly. And I'm sure that if we could hear him speak, we'd laugh at his accent and lack of proper English. Uneducated, poor, old, and out of work. That's how Shadrach died.

I hesitate telling you that story because of what you might think. Oh, I'm not worried about what you might think of poor Shadrach. I hesitate because of what you might think about *me*. You see, that man was my great-great-grandfather, my ancestor. I wish I could say (as my wife can) that I'm related to Benjamin Franklin, but my family tree has had more than its share of "rotten roots," some much worse off than Shadrach.

So that's my little family secret—that some of my relatives were uneducated, backwoods, dirt-poor hillbillies. It's the "skeleton" in my family closet.

And now you know.

But I'd like to tell you another secret. It's a family secret that's even more shocking than mine. In fact, I'm about to make a statement some people would consider inappropriate and disrespectful—maybe even blasphemous. It's something you may have never thought about before. But I think we know each other well enough now, so I'm gonna go ahead and say it. Here it is:

Jesus Christ has a skeleton in his closet.

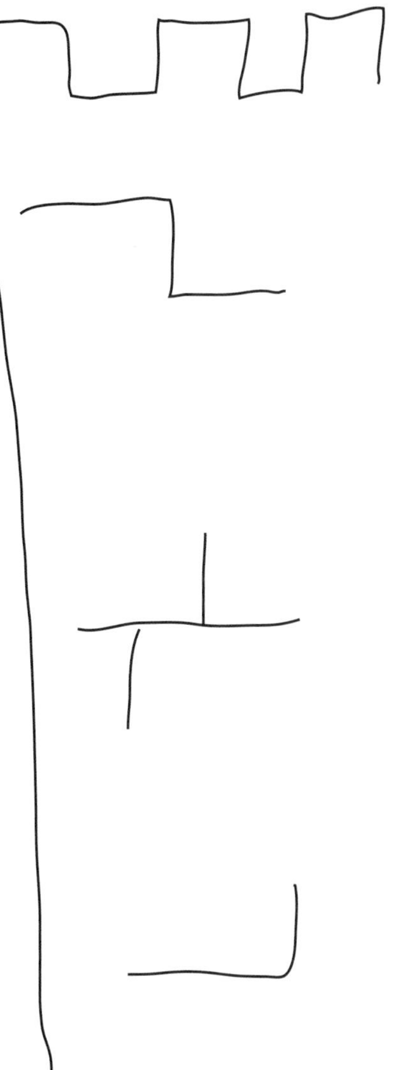

It's the kind of thing folks like us would rather keep hidden. It's something about Jesus' past—his family tree, to be exact. The fact is that Jesus' ancestry is marked by the stain of prostitution. That's right. The Son of God has an ancestor who was a member of humanity's oldest profession.

Surprisingly, Jesus isn't the least bit ashamed of her. This woman was King David's great-great-grandmother. And her remarkable story is the very reason that Christ is not embarrassed to be related to her.

THE WALL

Our story begins in the ancient city of Jericho roughly 3,500 years ago. This woman, Rahab, was scratching out a living as a prostitute. How she became a prostitute we don't know. However, since the beginning of time, human nature and the lust for sex haven't changed. In those days, weary travelers arriving in Jericho from far away places were greeted by females offering them sex for money. That was Rahab's business, and as the old saying goes, "business was good."

Jericho was a fortified city, meaning it had huge walls surrounding it. Those walls provided protection against foreign armies and invaders. We're not talking about juvenile delinquents destroying your mailbox or even a drive-by shooting. It was much worse than that. It was common for entire armies to come crashing down on your town unexpectedly—destroying the walls, burning

the houses, killing the men, and kidnapping or raping the women and girls.

Now you know why they had those huge walls.

In fact, the walls were so thick you could live *inside* them. Prostitutes' homes were often located on the wall. This way they could more easily lure travelers inside. It was the low-rent district. That's where Rahab lived, right near the front gate.

One day Rahab met two strangers at the gate and persuaded them to come home with her. Those two strangers turned out to be Israeli spies. After wandering around the desert for almost 40 years, General Joshua was ready to possess the land God had promised to them generations earlier. So he had

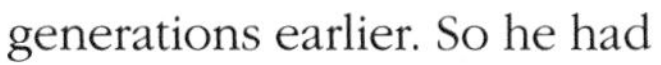

sent two undercover agents to check out the city and gather information useful in forming their battle plan.

Now you're probably wondering what two men from God's army were doing in the home of a prostitute, right? (If you're not wondering that, then pause and wonder about it right now…) Unfortunately, I don't have an answer for you. Maybe they figured they would stay under the radar in their clandestine mission by going home with a prostitute. In time of war, it pays to avoid being detected by the enemy! At any rate, they obviously intended their presence to remain a secret.

But somehow the news got out, reaching the ears of the King of Jericho. He promptly ordered Rahab to bring the men out to be executed as spies. Instead, she quickly hid the men, then lied to the king, saying they'd already left Jericho. He bought the lie, and later, at bedtime, Rahab went up to the roof, where she had hidden the spies. Once there, she made a surprising confession to them: "The Lord your God is God in heaven above and on earth below" (Joshua 2:11).

Basically, she confessed her belief that God had given the city into Israel's hands. Now think about that for a second. What a statement for a pagan, immoral, non-Jewish women to say! Suddenly, the pagan statuettes sitting silently on her shelf mean nothing to her. Years of living for herself, being used and abused by filthy, drunken men, had been suddenly replaced by a new pursuit—a belief that salvation belonged, not to some demon deity, but to the one true God.

This probably wasn't the first time she had heard of Israel's God. Jehovah's reputation had spread for decades, reaching Jericho and the surrounding land long before the two spies showed up. Jericho's inhabitants had heard about the Red Sea incident and how God had destroyed other armies who opposed Israel. Their hearts melted in fear of a God who could do this.

And so did Rahab's.

Her fear became a healthy motivation to survive the coming invasion by Israel. And when the spies let her in on their plans to destroy Jericho, she begged them to spare her family's lives.

In response to her hospitality, the men promised that she and her family would be spared when Israel destroyed Jericho. That same night, Rahab helped them escape by letting them down a scarlet rope on the city wall. They instructed Rahab to hang the same scarlet rope in her window to identify it when the invasion began, and to get her whole family inside the house. But if she mentioned any of this to anyone, she wouldn't be protected. So after sending them away, she *immediately* tied the scarlet rope to the window. Rahab wasn't taking any chances.

About a week later, Joshua's army crossed the Jordan River and the conquest began. When the men carrying the Ark of the Covenant set foot in the river, it instantly stopped flowing and backed up, just as it did 40 years earlier at the Red Sea. This was another visual reminder that God was still with them. The whole nation then crossed on dry ground.

In anticipation of the battle, Jericho was sealed tight. Nobody came in or left the city (Joshua 6:1). As for Israel, God had given Joshua a simple (but weird) plan (6:2-5). His army was to march around Jericho once a day for six days. The Ark would lead the advance, followed by seven priests carrying ram's horns, blowing as they marched.

They were instructed to march around the city seven times on the seventh day. Then, when the priests blew one long blast from their trumpets, everybody was to shout at the top of their lungs, and the walls would fall down. (Sure beats picking the lock on the front gate!)

This strange plan actually worked. After the city fell, Joshua gave instructions that Rahab and her family were to be spared, and she and her family were relocated to a place outside the camp of Israel (6:22-23). She went on to live with the people of Israel, eventually marrying and having a son, Boaz (6:25). Boaz married Ruth—whom you may have heard of. (She has a book of the Bible named after her.) They had a son, Obed, who had a son, Jesse. Jesse had several sons—one of them named David. And in case you're interested, you can trace the rest of the family tree in Matthew 1:6-17.

It ends with Jesus.

HEAVEN'S HARLOT

Okay, so let's stop and make a couple of observations. First, could you be any more insignificant than a prostitute living on a Palestinian wall in 1400 BC? I mean, c'mon. How much more of a loser could you be back then? Not only was it a decadent way to make a living, but it also it meant Rahab probably came from poverty. She had no social status. No pedigree. No class and obviously no morals. There were no health clinics in those days. No safe sex. Her possessions were likely little more than a bed, a scarlet sheet, and some cheap perfume—all "tools of the trade." She had probably never experienced love or real intimacy, but only the constant, deteriorating self-abuse that a life of prostitution brings. Rahab was a woman without a future. A woman without hope. A common tramp.

NIL

ZIP

She was nothing. ZERO NADA

But if living as a prostitute had taught her anything, it was how to survive. With no promise of tomorrow, her only job security lay in her ability to make another *sale*. But the day would come when her beauty would fade, and then where would she be? Alone, destitute, and desperate for food, she would be forced to join the band of beggars so plentiful in those days. Or worse, she would become a human scavenger, foraging for food in the city dump.

So when she heard about the coming invasion by the infamous Israelites, she realized that staying alive meant joining their side. While this was a logical decision, it meant abandoning her past and walking a new path. In Jericho, she had gained quite a reputation as a prostitute. With God's people, she would have the chance to start over, to make a brand new reputation. Though initially an outsider, she would eventually be known as the woman who had saved the spies, and in the process she saved herself. Perhaps in time, she would be accepted by the Jews and even considered a heroine of sorts for what she had done.

But there's a little more to it than that. According to the Bible, God saw more than what she *did* the night the spies came to visit her. Beyond just helping a couple of spies sneak out of town, she had confessed her belief in Jehovah as "God in heaven above and on earth below." That's what she'd come to believe in her heart. Helping the spies escape was more than just a way to keep her and her family from being destroyed. Her actions were an overflow of *her faith in God* (James 2:25). She believed Israel's God was the true God. She wanted to join his people and become a part of his family. Welcoming those spies into her home was a symbol she had welcomed the God of those spies into her heart.

God honored Rahab for her faith, including her in the lineage of Jesus Christ, declaring her to be righteous and even inducting her into the Hall of Faith (Hebrews 11:31).

But why? What was so great about Rahab's faith that pleased God so much? I believe it has something to do with *who* she was, *where* she was, and "*when*" she was.

Rahab was a harlot, a real low-lifer. She was living on a city wall targeted for demolition. And she lived during a time when you never knew when a band of radical fanatics would come charging over the hill against your village. There were no guarantees, no Homeland Security. Talk about the threat of terrorism! There was little you could do to protect or prepare yourself, especially if you lived on the wall! In such an attack, you were the first to die.

It was during this perilous time that Rahab decided to sink her faith into something secure. She knew she needed salvation, so she trusted God for safety and refuge—for salvation.

In Jehovah she recognized her only chance to better herself, benefit her family, and become somebody. She didn't have much, but she had the one thing that made all the difference in the world to God. She had *faith*. That was enough. Her trust in Jehovah was a grand-slam homer in the bottom of the ninth inning. Through faith, her stain of sin was washed away, her sleazy reputation replaced with a lasting legacy. What an example for us to follow! We may still call her "Rahab the Harlot"—but that's not what they call her in heaven.

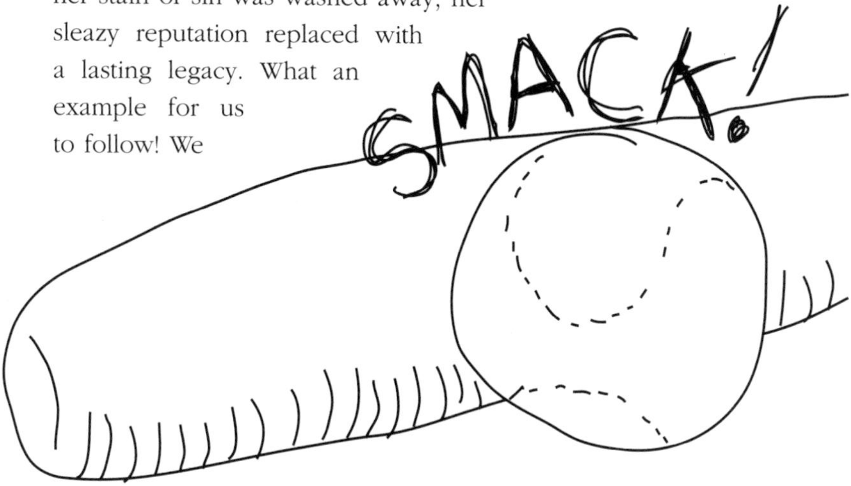

SMACK!

FROM "ZERO" TO "HERO"

So who are you? Are you a *nobody*? Hey, most of us around here are. This Losers Club you've joined contains a whole bunch of insignificant people. We're not movie legends or rock stars. We don't own private jets or second homes in Jamaica. We may not be first in our class or the best at anything. We fit the painted sign hanging on the door of a neighborhood tree house:

"Nobody act big. Nobody act small. Everybody just act medium."

That's what most members of this club are. Just regular people. Average. Ordinary. Common.

Medium.

If that describes you, be encouraged. It seems that God *really* enjoys hanging out with people like that.

> *Remember, dear brothers and sisters, that few of you were wise in the world's eyes, or powerful, or wealthy when God called you. Instead, God deliberately chose things the world considers foolish in order to shame those who think they are wise. And he chose those who are powerless to shame those who are powerful. God chose things despised by the world, things counted as nothing at all, and used them to bring to nothing what the world considers important, so that no one can ever boast in the presence of God. (1 Corinthians 1:26-29, NLT)*

God enjoys taking nobodies and transforming them into somebodies.

Society says in order to become somebody, you have to accomplish some great feat or record-breaking achievement. The world says to become significant, you have to "be Number 1." But God says you're *already* important in his eyes. All you have to do to achieve your greatest potential is to recognize him as Number 1. That's the big difference between God and the world.

Rahab teaches us that *no one* is beyond the reach of God's love. Her example also shows us it was just as hard to trust God back then as it is today. But even though a difficult choice, it was, and still is, the right one. Rahab got off the fence and chose God's side.

Are you straddling the fence? Do you really believe God's way is best for you?

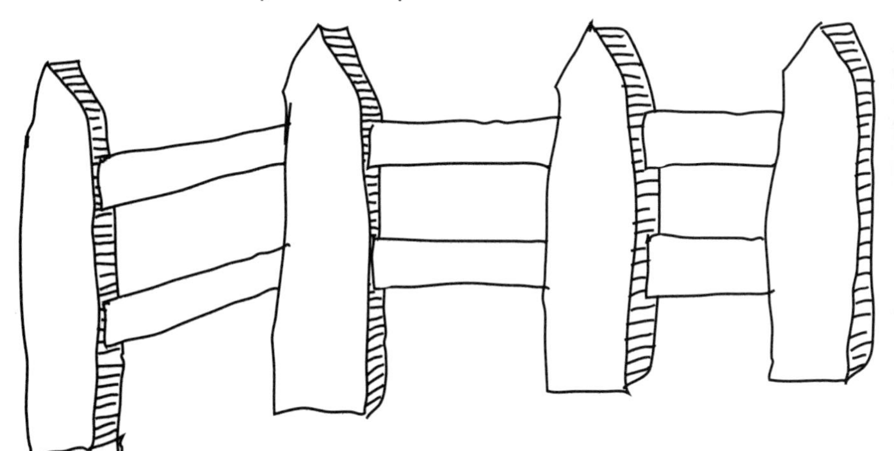

Rahab discovered the truth that "...without faith it is impossible to please God, because anyone who comes to him must believe that he exists and that he rewards those who earnestly seek him" (Hebrews 11:6). What about you? Do you believe that faith in God pays off somehow?

Though exercising faith may cost you at times, God is watching—and waiting—to reward you for trusting him with your life. It doesn't matter whether it's your city or your reputation that's under attack. If you choose to go with God, you'll save yourself a world of heartache and in the process find the way to live.

And that's something *your* descendants can be proud of.

So who are you? Are you a *nobody*? Hey, most of us around here are. This Losers Club you've joined contains a whole bunch of insignificant people. We're not movie legends or rock stars. We don't own private jets or second homes in Jamaica. We may not be first in our class or the best at anything.

Most of the members of this club are just regular people. Average. Ordinary. Common. If that describes you, be encouraged. It seems God *really* enjoys hanging out with people like that.

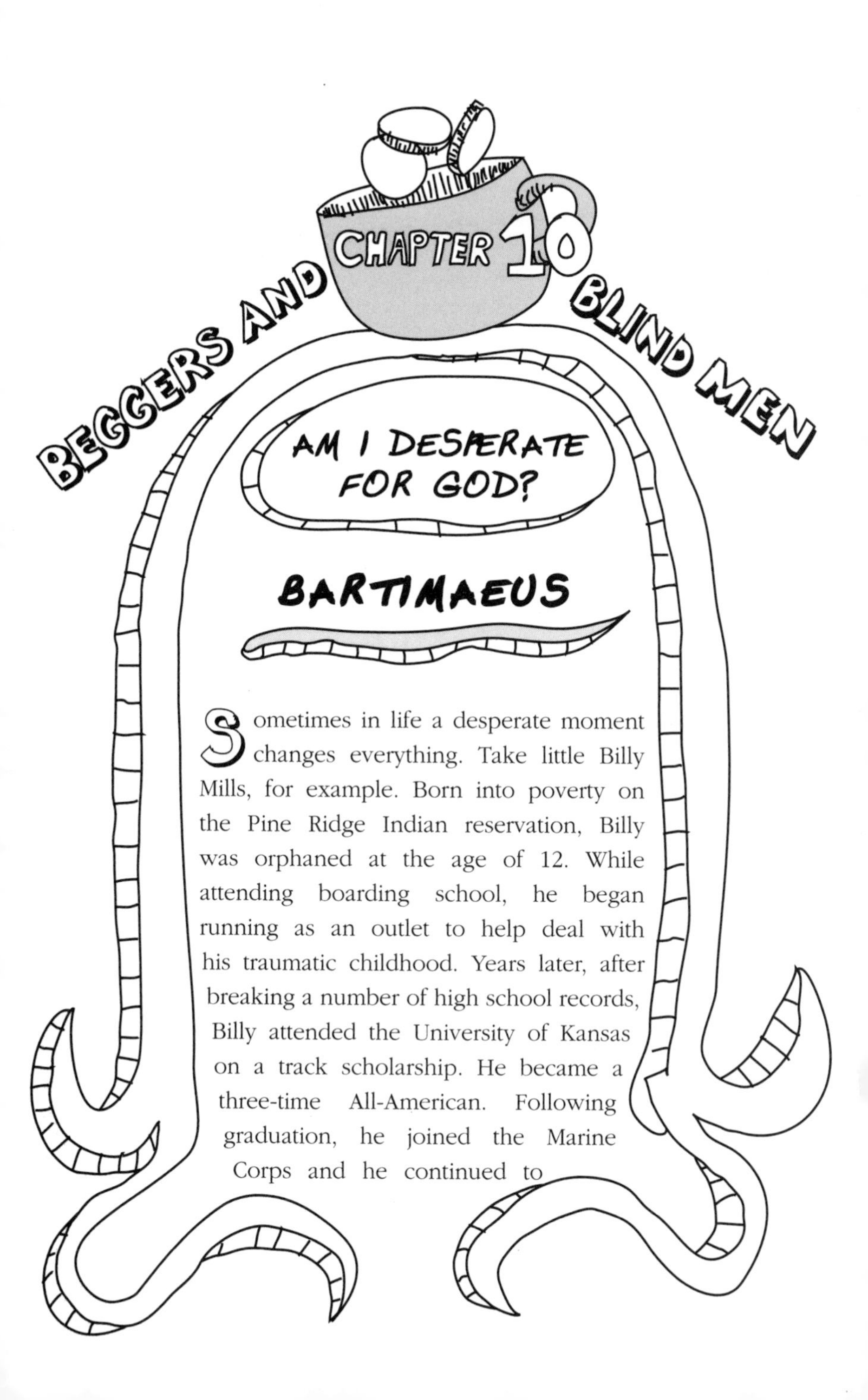

CHAPTER 10 BEGGERS AND BLIND MEN

AM I DESPERATE FOR GOD?

BARTIMAEUS

Sometimes in life a desperate moment changes everything. Take little Billy Mills, for example. Born into poverty on the Pine Ridge Indian reservation, Billy was orphaned at the age of 12. While attending boarding school, he began running as an outlet to help deal with his traumatic childhood. Years later, after breaking a number of high school records, Billy attended the University of Kansas on a track scholarship. He became a three-time All-American. Following graduation, he joined the Marine Corps and he continued to run, keeping up a rigorous 18-month training schedule or more than 100 miles per week. Billy's lifelong dream of Olympic glory came true when he was named to the 1964 U.S. Olympic team, qualifying for the 10,000 meters as well as the marathon.

One summer day in 1964, Billy found himself in Tokyo, Japan in the starting blocks of the 10,000-meter race. The gun sounded, and the six-mile race began. Mills was far from favored to win the event. His qualifying time was some 50 seconds slower than the time of Ron Clarke of Australia, the world record holder in the event. In addition, no American had ever won the 10,000 meters. The pre-media coverage focused almost entirely on Clarke and the other world-class runners, largely ignoring the Sioux Indian with the crewcut.

With one lap to go, Mills was still 15 meters behind the leaders. The race was all but over—or so everyone thought. It was a desperate moment for Mills. A time for opportunity. His one chance. His time. He was in the race of his life. Having endured racial slurs and predictions of failure by the experts, Billy knew that this moment only came along once in a lifetime. It was now or never. No second chance. There would be no gold or glory for second place. And Billy Mills knew it.

Reaching deep within, the 26-year-old former Marine found a reserve tank of energy stored for just such a time as this. Calling on every muscle in his body, Billy raced the final 100 yards, galloping like a thoroughbred. Passing Clarke and the pack, with agony etched on his face, Mills crossed the finish line, arms raised towards the sky in triumph. He had visualized breaking that finish line tape up to 75 times a day, and it had paid off. Mills won the gold, setting a new Olympic record in the process. His amazing come-from-behind finish is one of the greatest upsets in Olympic history.

Mills' victory was so unexpected that an Olympic official rushed up to the new champion and asked, "Who are you?" Just moments earlier no one had known his name. But from that day on, the whole world knew who Billy Mills was. To date, no other American has ever won the Olympic 10,000 meters. But on that summer day back in 1964, a Native-American orphan turned a moment of desperation into his moment of destiny.

RUNNING BLIND

Let me tell you about another man in the race of his life. This man wasn't in the Olympics, or even in a literal footrace. His name was Bartimaeus, and he lived a long time ago. Now Bart had two strikes against him. First, he was blind. Second, he was a poor beggar. And those things proved to be huge handicaps in his race. Add the fact that he was probably homeless as well, and—well, let's just say the odds weren't in his favor.

Of course, Bart didn't plan to become a beggar. It wasn't his chosen profession. I mean, it's not as if he went to "Beggar's School." Bart couldn't help being blind, a condition that prevented him from having a real job. No alternative employment options were available in those days. A beggar's life back then was even more difficult than it is now. At least today we have homeless shelters and government programs to assist those in need. In Jesus' day, there were no welfare checks or government handouts. No Salvation Army. No allowances for those with handicaps in first century Palestine. No Braille menus or seeing-eye dogs. Without relatives to care for you, you had only one option.

Begging.

Put yourself in this man's sandals. You're blind. Darkness is your best friend. Your other senses compensate for your lack of sight. It's like playing basketball with four players after the fifth man has fouled out. The other players have to fill in the gap. You "see" the world through sound, touch, and smell. You sit by the roadside all day, head slightly raised, straining to hear and sense where people are. Your hands are lifted with open palms as you solicit coins from strangers. You hear the shuffling of feet as traffic passes by. Your ears perk up at the sound of jingling change in their pockets, followed by that clinking sound coins make as they're tossed into your lap. Your finely tuned sense of hearing helps you distinguish the sound of one coin from another.

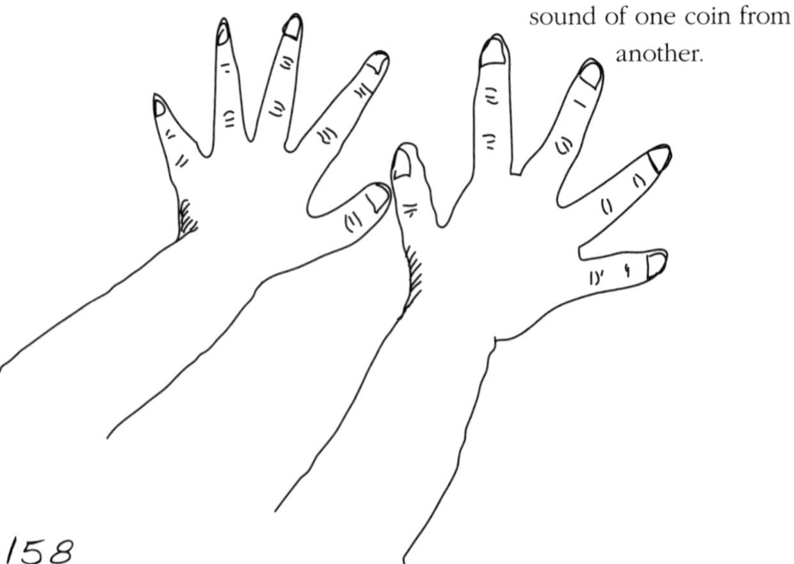

Blindness has also heightened your sense of touch. It's a flashlight in your world of darkness. It's your way of mapping out things and people—a job normally reserved for your eyes. Hearing helps you size up a situation, even enabling you to feel your way home at night. Partnering with that acute ability is your sense of smell. You can tell what's cooking around the comer, or if a woman wearing perfume is near.

OBEY YOUR THIRST

Sitting by the roadside one day, Bartimaeus sensed that something big was happening. He heard a huge crowd coming his way, and that might mean he would make some money. For "Blind Bart," the shuffling of feet was the sweet sound of opportunity knocking.

As he prepared himself for another round of begging that day, Bart heard something he'd never heard before. Conversations buzzed with news of a healer. While he'd heard rumors like that before, this time was different. People were saying this man was no sleight-of-hand-magician or back alley witch doctor. They claimed he was the Jewish Messiah, the One for whom Israel had waited centuries. The "Son of David," they called him. The heavenly heir to King David's throne. God had promised this Anointed One, or Christ, would someday deliver Israel from sin and reign over God's people forever.

Though he couldn't see, Bart must have listened well in "Saturday school" at the temple growing up. The moment he heard who Jesus was, he began crying out, "Son of David, have mercy on me" (Mark 10:47). He cried mercy, knowing that was precisely what he needed.

Bart knew God didn't *owe* him anything. He understood the ability to see was not a right we inherit but rather a privilege we enjoy. Aware he was in no position to demand healing from God, he begged for it.

He was good at begging.

Of course, if he'd been a prominent member of society, people would've cleared a way for him to get to Jesus. But just the opposite occurred. The crowd began verbally abusing him, discouraging his efforts to reach Christ. *Shut up,* they advised him (Mark 10:48). *You're not important enough for the Teacher to stop his important business and pay attention to you. Just who do you think you are?*

But Bart ignored the crowd. In fact, he didn't really care at all what others thought or said. He had lived way too long in total darkness. His desire to meet Jesus was greater than his desire for acceptance from the crowd. His need was more important than their words. He felt a sense of urgency that day, thirsting for something more than a few pennies. He recognized Jesus could offer him something this world could not. So eager was he to have contact with Jesus that he raised his voice even louder, drowning out the jeers and cheers of the huge crowd. Bartimaeus was motivated, determined that nothing was going to keep him from Jesus.

He was *desperate.*

Let's switch the focus for a second. What stops *you* from getting close to Jesus? Does it matter to you what other people think? And if so, why? What does "the crowd" give you that's so much better than what Christ offers? Acceptance? Security? Love? Have you ever recognized your need for Jesus? Have you ever considered how much you are in need of his mercy? Most of us are not physically blind, but there are some things in life worse than not having sight. God says that because of our thoughts, words, and actions, we don't deserve heaven or salvation (Romans 3:23). In fact, our very nature makes us unworthy (Romans 7:18). The only thing left for God to do is punish us (Romans 6:23). The more we understand this truth, the more we, too, will cry out for mercy. Like Bart, we need an attitude that says: *Lord, please don't give me what I deserve. Instead, please touch my heart and heal me from sin.*

That's where Bartimaeus was coming from. That was his prayer, a prayer that reaches God's ears *every* time. Jesus' policy is never to turn away anyone who cries out to him, so he immediately stopped and called for Bartimaeus (Mark 10:49).

In his enthusiasm, Bart jumped up and ran to Jesus, leaving his cloak behind (10:50).

"What do you want me to do for you?" Jesus said.

"Rabbi," Bartimaeus responded, "I want to see" (10:51).

Notice he didn't ask Jesus for money. Did he need cash? Uh...yeah! And Jesus could have given that to him. He could have turned rocks into riches. But again, this man was focusing on his greatest need. He didn't bring to Jesus a list of ten demands, or even three wishes. His request was singular and simple. "Lord, I want to see."

FLIPPING THE LIGHT SWITCH

The crowd stood in silence, eagerly awaiting Jesus' response. Some fixed their gaze on Christ, while others

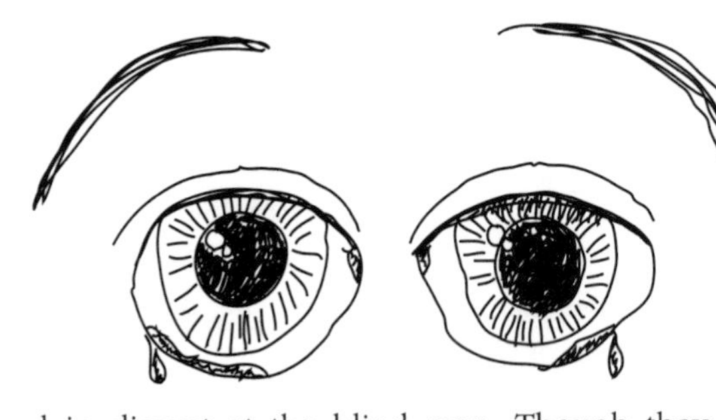

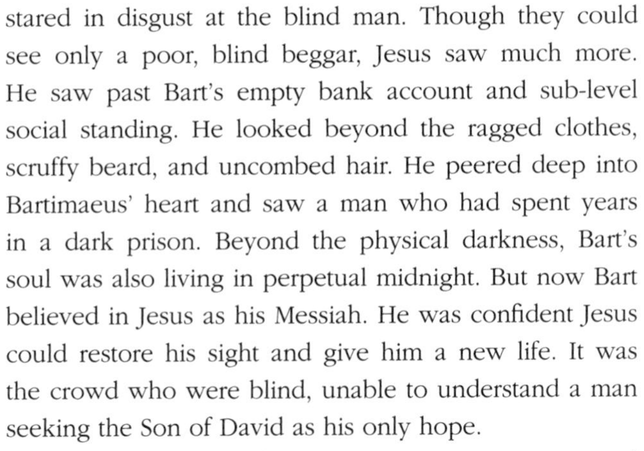

stared in disgust at the blind man. Though they could see only a poor, blind beggar, Jesus saw much more. He saw past Bart's empty bank account and sub-level social standing. He looked beyond the ragged clothes, scruffy beard, and uncombed hair. He peered deep into Bartimaeus' heart and saw a man who had spent years in a dark prison. Beyond the physical darkness, Bart's soul was also living in perpetual midnight. But now Bart believed in Jesus as his Messiah. He was confident Jesus could restore his sight and give him a new life. It was the crowd who were blind, unable to understand a man seeking the Son of David as his only hope.

Upon hearing the man's request, Jesus was moved with compassion. Moved deep inside with a love for this poor man, he reached out to do his favorite thing—*touch* (Matthew 20:34). Specifically, he touched Bart's eyes. Then Jesus said, "Go, your faith has healed you" (Mark 10:52).

And love rained down.

Immediately and miraculously, Bart's sight was restored. Squinting at the sunlight for perhaps the very first time, the first thing Bart saw was the silhouette of the Merciful One. Bartimaeus' new eyes met Jesus' eyes, seeing in them something most don't expect to find in the eyes of God. He saw in Jesus understanding and compassion.

And tears.

Just minutes before, he could only dream of what Jesus of Nazareth might look like. Now Bartimaeus was no doubt greeted with a huge smile beaming from the healer's face. He had found more than physical deliverance through Jesus. He had also been granted acceptance into heaven and into the presence of God. Bart began a whole new life.

It's interesting that Jesus didn't begin making demands of the former blind man. We might imagine he would say more. *Bartimaeus, now that you're a believer, this begging business will have to stop. And you'll need to get some new clothes. I can't have my people looking like beggars.*

There is no need for any of that. Jesus didn't have to command Bart to follow him or change his lifestyle. It happened naturally. Bartimaeus immediately began glorifying God and following Jesus. Why? Because he understood what had happened to him. Others also praised God because of him.

Ever wonder why some people seem to be so in love with God? Ever wonder how they got that way?

I believe it's because of their G.Q.—their "Gratitude Quotient." People who have a sense of their bad condition without Christ tend to appreciate salvation more. And that gratitude produces a natural love for God.

Suppose that you are sunbathing in the pool one July afternoon, and you ask a friend to toss you a raft. "Thanks," you respond, and then you return to your dreamwork beneath your shades.

Now suppose you unintentionally insult a girl whose dad happens to be the boss of the Gambino crime family. Suddenly, you find yourself 30 miles out into the Pacific Ocean, with chains and concrete blocks secured to your body! What then? Let me spell it out for you:

Y-O-U A-R-E G-O-I-N-G D-O-W-N!

Think you might feel kinda desperate as you swallow your first mouthful of seawater? Okay, *now* call out to someone for a "flotation device." Cry for help *now*. What's the tone of your voice? Do you whisper that request or shout it out loud? Think you can live without that life raft? (There's a reason they call it a *life* raft.) And let's suppose someone tosses you a raft. What kind of thanks will you express now? How do you feel toward the one who just saved your life?

A little more thankful now, perhaps? And why? Why are you now bonded to that person for life? Because you understand how bad off you were in the water. You recognize the helplessness of your condition. Being saved from that awful fate automatically, *naturally* produces a love inside for that person. Your *desperation* naturally leads to your *devotion*.

Truth is, people who understand what they were without Christ are drawn like a magnet to a relationship with him. They know how much better off they are with God in their life. And they love him for it. Jesus put it this way, "He who has been forgiven little loves little" (Luke 7:47). The opposite is also true—those who realize how much they have been forgiven, love much. Bartimaeus figured: *Hey, if he cares enough to do this for me, there is nothing I won't do for him!*

Bartimaeus knew who he was, and he also knew who Jesus was. By simply placing his trust in Christ to meet his need, he experienced the Savior's healing power.

WINNING THE RACE

If you were to make a list of the ten greatest Bible characters, Bartimaeus probably wouldn't make the cut. In fact, he might not even make the "Top 20." Bart hasn't gotten a lot of press over the years. After all, his entire story only takes up a few verses, right? He's a virtual nobody.

So why did God decide to include him in the Bible? I think he's there because of what he teaches us. And what would that be? Simply that when we run to Christ in need, he responds with understanding, compassion, and healing. When we are willing to do anything to get to him, he joyfully reaches out and touches us. And that touch always makes a difference—a difference you can *see*. A difference that makes you see life from a new perspective. It's not a difference you have to create. Not something you have to work up. It's a difference he creates in you.

Have you felt that difference?

As you sit reading, Jesus once again is passing by—this time through the pages of this chapter. This then becomes *your* moment—your opportunity to cry out to the Savior. Is there a blindness or some other spiritual need in your life? Where are you in the race? Do you feel like giving up? Are you hurting from the agony life can bring? Where do you need his power today? Are you willing to cry out, regardless of what the crowd might think? Or will you allow what others may say to keep you from him?

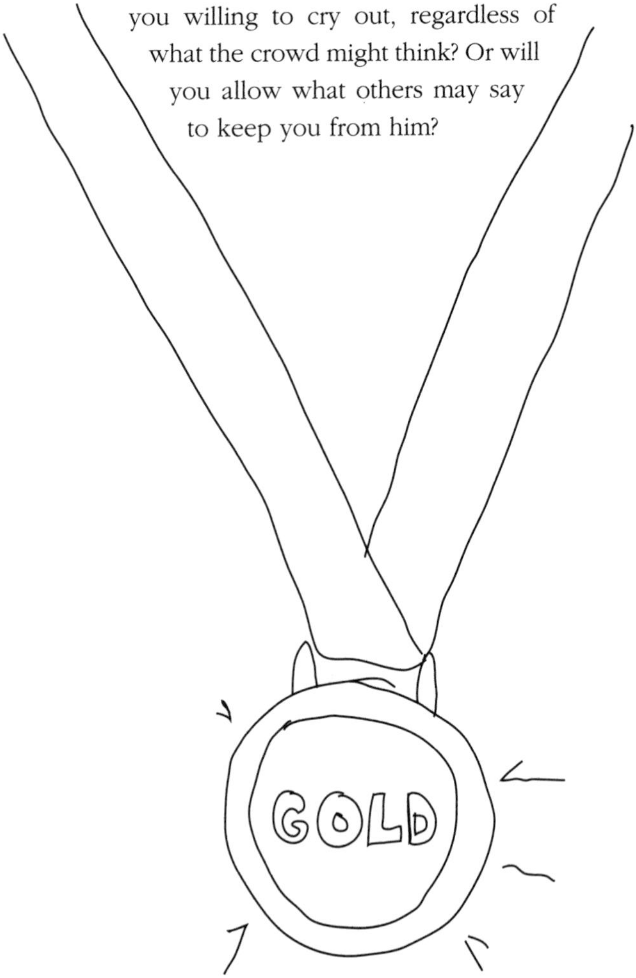

GOLD

Know this: Jesus will stop and speak to you. He understands everything about you. And if you call on him in faith, he is eager to heal you.

So stop begging. Listen. Get up and follow your ears. He's waiting.

By the way, when you complete your race and arrive in heaven, look for Bartimaeus. Oh, you'll have no problem spotting him. He'll be the guy at the finish line, leaping and dancing like he's just won a gold medal.

Bartimaeus was determined nothing would keep him away from Jesus.

What about you? What stops you from getting close to Jesus? Is it "the crowd" that surrounds you? Where do you need his power today? Are you willing to cry out, regardless of what the crowd might think?

Know this: If you call on Jesus, he will stop and speak to you. He is eager to heal you.

CHAPTER 11

CLOSER THAN A BROTHER

WHAT KIND OF FRIEND AM I?

ARISTARCHUS

It's the phone call you *never* want to get.

I was at a fundraiser for missions when my cell phone rang. It was bad news. *Really* bad news. One of the high school girls in my ministry had been killed in an auto accident. And of all people, it was Elizabeth.

Now, you have to understand who this girl was. Beautiful. Funny. Athletic. Musical. Daring. The life of any party. Did I mention "beautiful"? That was Elizabeth. She was the total package, and so much fun to be around! She would do virtually anything on a dare.

Kiss a pig? "Sure! Where is he?"

Wrestle her sisters in the middle of the youth room floor? No problem.

Run for student body president…and win? Done.

Enter and be elected Homecoming Queen? Mission accomplished.

Hold down a part-time job at a local radio station? No big deal.

Challenge any guy in youth group to an arm-wrestling match…and win? Most every time.

Light up a room just by walking through the door? Every time.

So you can understand my shock and disbelief when I heard she was gone. I was devastated. Immediately, I thought of her family. This would be crushing news to her sisters. And I could hardly even imagine what her mom must be feeling. So my best friend, Joel, and I jumped into my car and raced over to Elizabeth's house. By the time we arrived, people were already gathering.

Making our way back to the bedroom, we opened the door to see her mom sitting alone on the bed in the dark. As the hallway light illuminated the room, I saw her dad there as well. It was obvious they had been crying. The grief was already etching itself into the mother's face. Had a thought bubble been hovering over my head, it would have read: *What on earth am I going to say to a woman who has just lost her precious daughter?*

Who can understand such things? Not me. And so, walking over, I sat down, placed my arm around her, looked her in the eyes and said, "We love you."

That was all I knew to say. There was nothing else I could say. It was all I had. And so we sat in dark silence for what seemed like 30 minutes. What she needed from me in that moment wasn't answers. She didn't need me to try to explain why God had allowed this awful thing to happen to her 17-year-old. She didn't need me to toss Bible verses at her. She didn't need to hear me say everything was going to be all right. What she needed in that moment was a friend.

Nothing more.

A few days later, I spoke at Elizabeth's funeral. In addition to hundreds of church members, more than one thousand teenagers poured into our church that day—nearly the entire student body of Elizabeth's high school. I shared the love of Jesus with those students and the hope of eternal life he offered them. I said what I knew Elizabeth would want me to say. I also comforted the family with the assurance that they would see Elizabeth again. And though I was "the minister" that day, I was again, more than anything, just a friend.

I admit, I'm not the smartest man in the world. But I do try to pay attention. And I've observed that life often brings pain, sadness, and grief. There are times when living is simply no fun. Sometimes it actually stinks! During those down times, you need someone who'll stick with you no matter what. You need people who'll stand by your side, even if it means risking a lot. Friends who are willing to sit beside you when you're hurting and not say a word. Just by being there, they've said all they need to say.

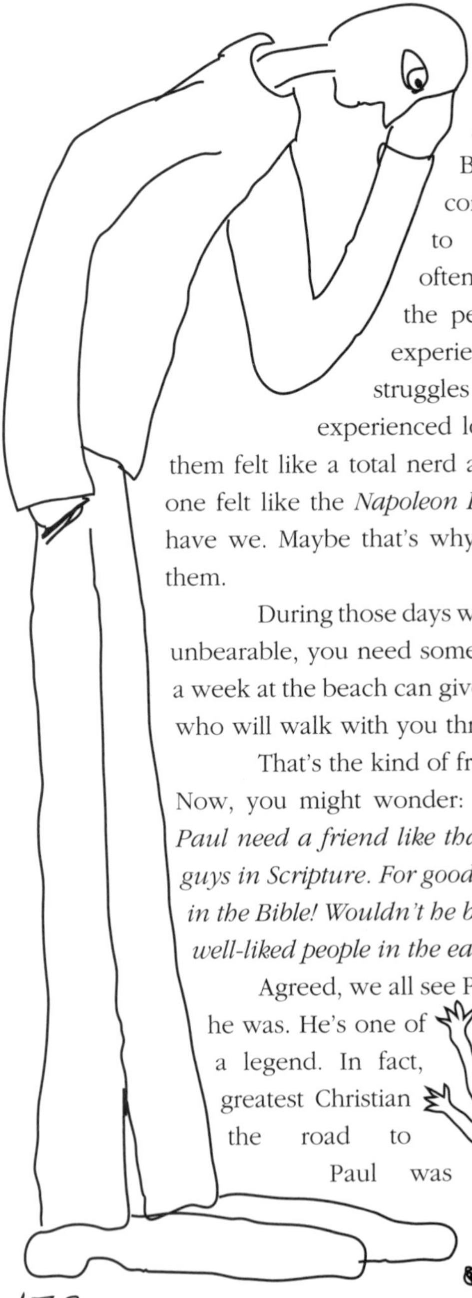

HEBREW HIT MAN

By now, I hope this book has convinced you that, contrary to the super-saint image we often have of Bible characters, the people who fill the Scriptures experienced the same hardships and struggles we face. Every one of them experienced loss and failure. Every one of them felt like a total nerd at one time or another. Every one felt like the *Napoleon Dynamite* of the day. And so have we. Maybe that's why it's so easy to identify with them.

During those days when the pain of living is nearly unbearable, you need something neither a painkiller nor a week at the beach can give you. You need a friend. One who will walk with you through life's worst moments.

That's the kind of friend the apostle Paul needed. Now, you might wonder: *Why would the great apostle Paul need a friend like that? He's one of the most godly guys in Scripture. For goodness' sakes, he wrote 13 books in the Bible! Wouldn't he be one of the most popular and well-liked people in the early church?*

Agreed, we all see Paul as a giant of the faith. And he was. He's one of the *biggies* of Christianity, a legend. In fact, he may have been the greatest Christian who ever lived. But the road to legendary status for Paul was paved with hardship and pain—*lots* of it.

For starters, Paul had to overcome a really bad reputation with those early Christians. If you'll recall, earlier in his life, Paul was one of the main guys responsible for hunting down Christians, arresting them, and putting them to death. In fact, he was present the first time a Christian was executed—and he was cheering on the executioners (Acts 7:58; 8:1).

It got worse from there. He went from simply being a foot soldier in the war against Christians to becoming the "Fuehrer of the Religious Gestapo." He was a bounty hunter. A one-man posse. He ran his own *murder factory*. We have no record of how many believers were killed under his command, but we know the number was high enough to make Christians run and hide when they heard his name mentioned. So you can understand why the early Christians were a little skeptical when "Dr. Death" showed up at church. And that's when Barnabas stepped in to vouch for him (Acts 9:26-27).

Now, you might think Paul's problems would be solved following his dramatic conversion to Christianity, but just the opposite occurred. Oh sure, the church slowly began accepting him,

but his old Pharisee fraternity brothers weren't too excited about his new faith. In fact, they were fit to be tied. Why? Paul had changed teams in the middle of the season. He had sneaked across enemy lines, switching sides during a time of war. Paul (formerly Saul) became the number 1 bad guy on Israel's "Most Wanted" list. They hired hit men to "rub him out." Heck, they hired hit *mobs*. Everywhere Paul went, he encountered fanatics who were ready and willing to end his life. In addition to trying to kill him, they also infiltrated churches to undermine his authority and teaching. These guys were ruthless, stopping at nothing in their efforts to ruin Paul.

Paul's misfortune didn't stop there (as if that weren't enough!). In addition to hit squads and smear campaigns, Paul suffered a lot of other things on his rocky road to Christian celebrity status. 2 Corinthians 11:24-28 gives us a glimpse of some of the things Paul endured because of his dedication to spread the Gospel. He was

- Whipped with 39 lashes. The Jews did this to him five times...in the synagogue!
- Beaten with rods. Big nightsticks or "billy-clubs." This happened three times.
- Stoned "to death." Or at least so bloodied and mangled the mob thought he was dead.
- Shipwrecked. He had to tread water for 24 hours in the open sea.
- Constantly traveling. (Trust me. This one will wear you out.)
- In constant danger from rivers, robbers, religious zealots, and Romans. Paul always had to look over his shoulder.

-  Exhausted from hard work and lack of sleep.
- Deprived of food and drink for long periods.
- Without shelter, spending many cold nights sleeping under the open sky.
- Under daily emotional, mental, and spiritual stress from caring for all the churches.

Of course, aside from these things, Paul had it easy! Answering God's call on his life meant traveling a rough road. He paid a price for his commitment to Jesus.
So here's the $100 question: *Did Paul have anybody with him during those times?*

The answer is *yes*. Paul was fortunate to have traveling companions and ministry partners who rode out a bunch of storms with him. They were buddies who were willing to hang with him, no matter how bad things got. Among this Band of Brothers were Dr. Luke (who wrote the Gospel of Luke and the Book of Acts), Tychichus (a good servant to Paul), Onesimus (a former slave), Mark (see Chapter 8), Justus (real name Jesus), Epaphras (a prayer warrior), and Aristarchus (from Thessalonica). If we knew more background info on these guys, we could write several books and make a mini-series based on their adventures. But I have only one chapter, so I want to tell you about just one of these awesome men: Aristarchus.

CROWD SURFING

Now, I'm betting that you've never heard of this guy—and I'm positive you don't have any friends named after him. But Aristarchus was a devoted follower of Christ who at some point joined Paul's traveling team. Paul may have led him to Christ in Thessalonica during a time when it was very unpopular to be a Christian. The civilized world was in total spiritual darkness, having not yet heard the name of Jesus. So everywhere Paul went, he broke new ground for the Gospel—make that he *took* new ground. His missionary work was more like war as he entered cities deeply rooted in pagan worship. This was Satan's territory. *His* real estate. Every city and province was under his control. So as people began turning to Christ, their old ways had to go. For some, this life change affected their incomes and livelihoods, especially those who made their living from pagan practices. For example, in Ephesus, a group of sorcerers who came to Christ brought all their witchcraft materials and sorcery scrolls together, making a huge bonfire with them (no "s'mores"). Someone standing by calculated the value of those scrolls to be fifty thousand *drachmas*, or about $2 million! That got the attention of some other businessmen in the community.

One of them was a silversmith named Demetrius, who made little silver shrines of Artemis (one of their main gods). He called a meeting of his idol-making friends and argued that Paul's preaching had to stop because Artemis was in danger of being "robbed of her divine majesty" (Acts 19:23-27). That got a hearty "Amen." Then he added that they all might lose their jobs, as Paul's "Gospel campaign" was bad for their economy. And he was partly right. The meeting turned into a free-for-all, Paul-bashing session. The noise level grew and the crowd swelled. The small town business meeting was now a citywide event. Then things got ugly.

That's when a riot broke out.

Perhaps you've heard the term "mob rule" used to describe what happens when a crowd gets out of control. Put simply, a mob will do together what individuals would rarely do by themselves. Mobs will loot, rob, set fire to buildings, fight police, destroy neighborhoods, and attack innocent citizens. When that happens, be afraid. Be very afraid.

Mob rule is when 75,000 European soccer fans decide to protest the outcome of a match and people end up dead. It's when 10,000 concertgoers push closer to the stage and someone gets crushed. It's when fire breaks out in a nightclub and dozens get trampled. It's insanity on parade. That's mob rule.

And that's what happened in Ephesus. Frustrated and white-hot with anger, the crowd seized two of Paul's traveling companions—Gaius and our man, Aristarchus—and dragged them into the theater (or perhaps passed them over their heads). It was mass confusion and chaos. Paul wasn't there, but when he heard the news he immediately tried to go and help. However, his Christian friends wouldn't let him. (Acts 19:29-31)

For two hours, the angry mob repeatedly shouted, "Great is Artemis of the Ephesians!" Two solid hours they shouted this! (Obsessed, are ya?) (Acts 19:34) Meanwhile, Aristarchus was held hostage, not knowing whether at any moment he might be stoned, handcuffed and thrown off a building, or simply torn apart like a paper towel. In any case, he and Gaius had some time to think about the dangers of being Paul's friends.

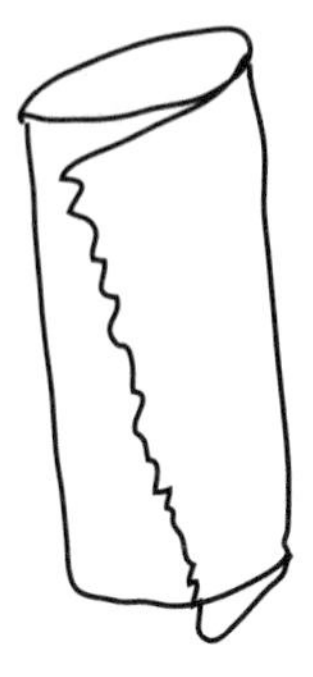

Fortunately, a city official eventually took charge, calming the crowd and warning them that the Romans

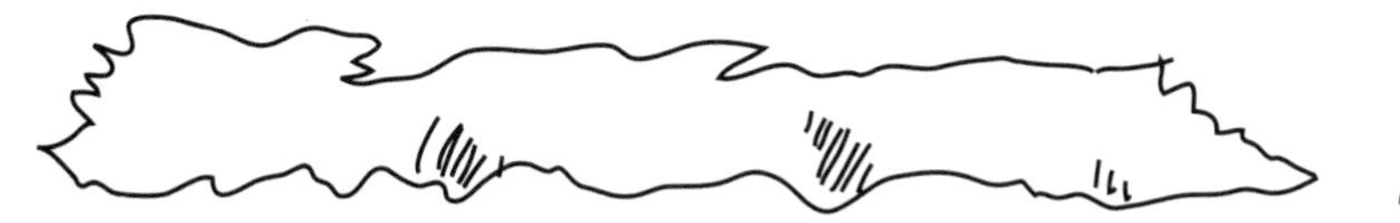

might arrest them all for causing a needless riot. So they all went home. Just like that. Go figure!

So Paul gathered the team and left for Greece. While there, they learned of an assassination plot, so Paul sent his friends on ahead to get the heat off them (Acts 20:5).

Riots. Assassination plots. Uncertainty. Traveling with Paul back then was like publicly preaching the Gospel in some radical Muslim countries today. Sound dangerous?

But in spite of these risks, Aristarchus didn't bail. He stayed with Paul.

"I GOT YOUR BACK"

Years later, we find Aristarchus still traveling with Paul—town to town, region to region—spreading the news the world was waiting to hear: news of love, forgiveness, and eternal life through Jesus Christ. But Aristarchus never considered a career change. His job with Paul gave him more adventure and challenge in a few years than most people experience in a lifetime. Never knowing what to expect whenever they entered a town, they had to be prepared to face either a reception committee or a riot.

Over time the pair covered a lot of geography together. (If only they had had "frequent *sailing* miles" back then!) Aristarchus understood that working as a missionary with the apostle Paul wasn't a profession that promised wealth, health benefits, or many perks. Quite the opposite. Being with Paul meant experiencing the same hardships Paul encountered. Aristarchus collected his share of missionary scars. But it was worth it for the sake of the Gospel. And it was worth it for his friend Paul, the man who had first shared the good news with him back home in Thessalonica.

Aristarchus owed Paul. So he watched out for him. Stood *by* him. Stood *with* him. Stood *for* him. There's no doubt that Aristarchus would have sacrificed his life for Paul. Because of Aristarchus' faith in Christ, he instinctively knew what Jesus meant when he told his disciples, "Greater love has no one than this, that one lay down his life for his friends" (John 15:13). Aristarchus took care of Paul, or as we say today...*he had his back.*

Paul followed Christ, and so did Aristarchus, so he had no problem following Paul wherever he went. It had long been Paul's desire to take the Gospel to Rome, the hub of first-century civilization. Paul knew if the seed of the Gospel were planted in Rome, it could spread wherever the Roman Empire expanded—to Spain and further, to new countries. Believers in those countries could take the Gospel to the rest of the world. That was Paul's way of thinking, and Rome was the key to his vision.

By the way, check your history. That's exactly what happened. From Rome, the Gospel did go north, to Spain and beyond. Eventually it reached what is now England. From there it crossed over to a tiny new experiment in colonization called "America."

And here we are.

CELLMATES

When Paul finally made it to Rome, he wasn't visiting as a tourist—strolling the streets, gawking at architecture, and snapping pictures with a disposable camera. Instead, his arrival in Italy's capital quickly led to chains around his neck. Arrested for preaching and being an all-around "trouble maker," Paul spent the next several years in a prison cell. He would never see the rest of Europe. In fact, he would never leave Rome. His travel days were officially over. It was time to retire his suitcase. He would spend his final days of life in jail.

But while Caesar could keep him a prisoner, the emperor was powerless to contain the spread of Paul's fiery faith. From his cell, the apostle penned several "harmless" letters. Addressed to friends in cities scattered across Asia Minor, his correspondence ignited the spread of Christianity worldwide. You can find those letters in your own Bible. And 2,000 years later, they continue to bring God's truth to us.

Of course, Paul had no way of knowing his writings would have this effect on the world. He was stuck in prison awaiting either appeal or execution, not knowing whether he would live or die. But at least he had friends like Aristarchus by his side.

Okay, so why is Aristarchus in the Losers Club? Well, we don't know of any great sermons he preached or any books he wrote. He never set a world record or recorded a number 1 hit. He really was a *nobody*. Just a travel companion. A fellow worker and fellow prisoner. A faithful laborer. He didn't really do anything in life other than stay close to Paul and be his friend.

But that's exactly why he's part of the club.

That's what qualifies him as a fellow loser.

As you pass through this short life, some of your friends will be classmates. Others will be teammates or work associates. But when it's all said and done, when your traveling days are over, you'll look back and realize that only a precious few of those friends were true "cellmates." You'll realize that without them, you wouldn't be the person you've become.

May I make a suggestion? Don't wait until you're in a prison cell waiting, not knowing whether you'll be pardoned or put under the sword. Today, treasure the friends God has given you. Right now, thank him for that small band of believers who, if necessary, would walk through fire with you. Better yet, why not become that kind of friend to others—dependable, faithful, loyal, a constant source of encouragement.

In doing so, you'll be a lot like Aristarchus: a friend closer than a brother.

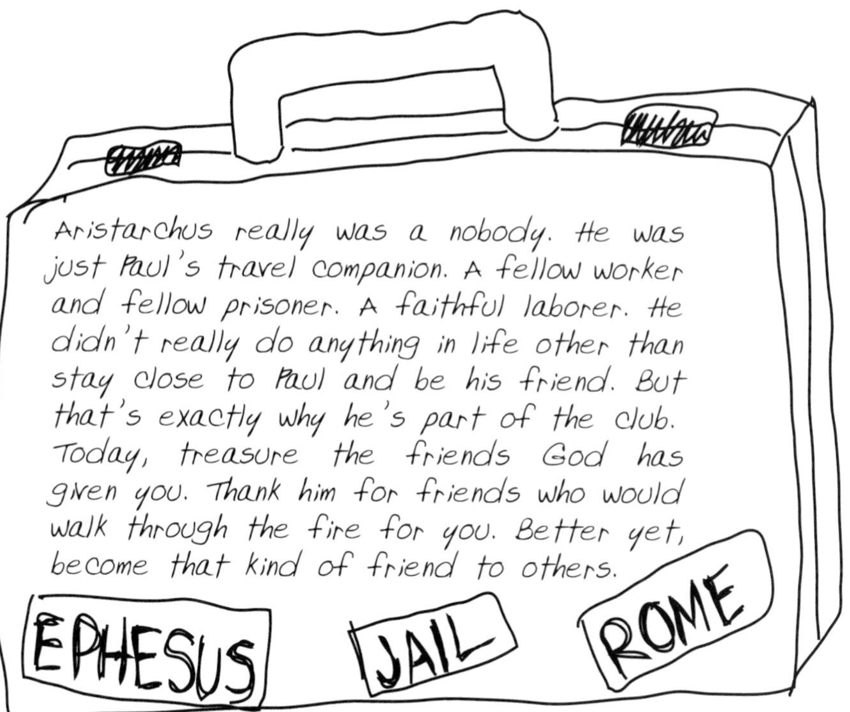

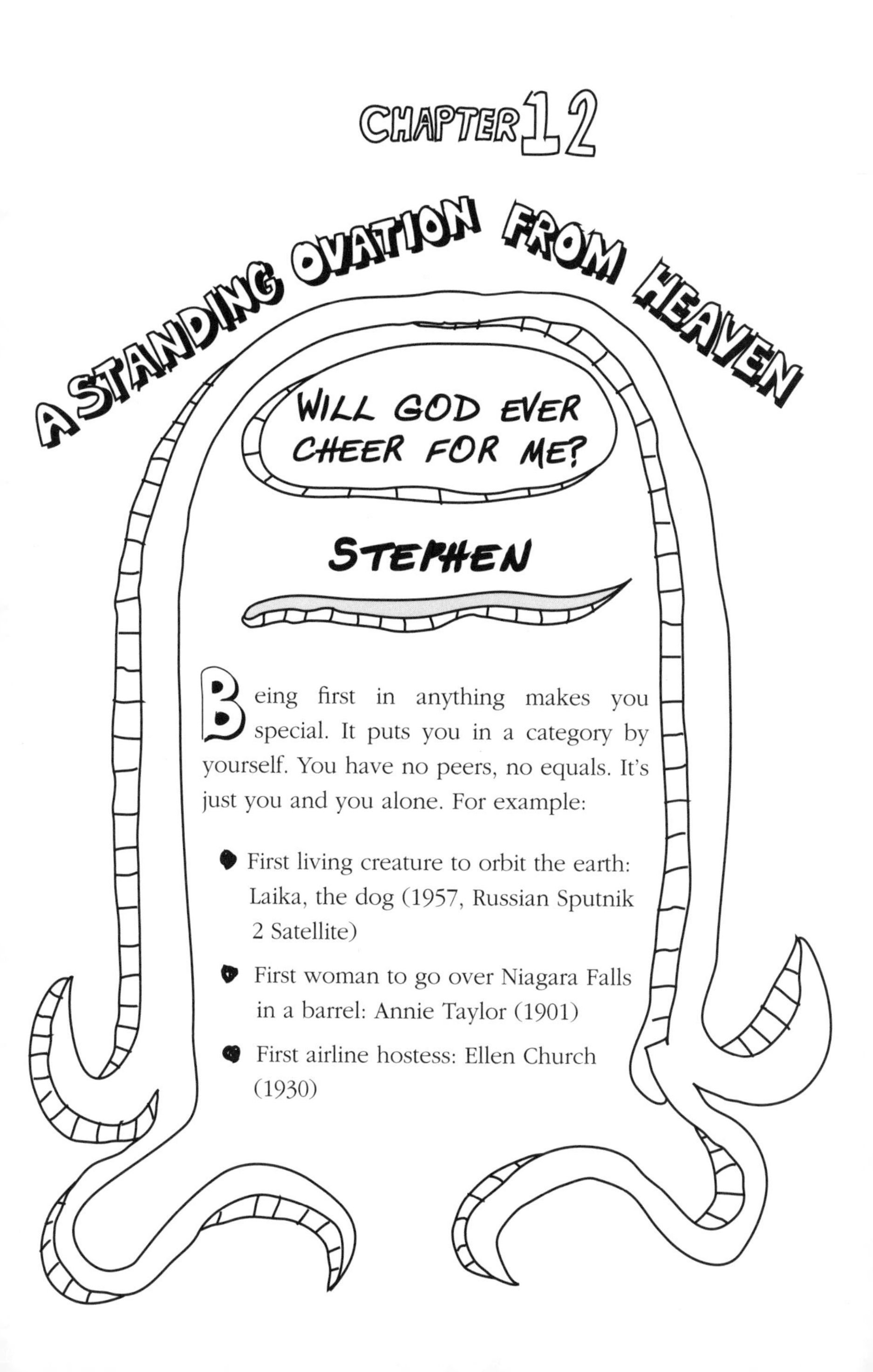

CHAPTER 12

A STANDING OVATION FROM HEAVEN

WILL GOD EVER CHEER FOR ME?

STEPHEN

Being first in anything makes you special. It puts you in a category by yourself. You have no peers, no equals. It's just you and you alone. For example:

- First living creature to orbit the earth: Laika, the dog (1957, Russian Sputnik 2 Satellite)
- First woman to go over Niagara Falls in a barrel: Annie Taylor (1901)
- First airline hostess: Ellen Church (1930)

- First boy to reach the rank of Eagle Scout: Arthur R. Eldred (1912)
- First Miss America: 16-year-old Margaret German (1921)
- First animal to be cloned: Dolly, the lamb (1996)

Feel smarter now? Enlightened? Impressed? Ready for a round of *Jeopardy*? Okay, maybe these belong to the "Who Cares?" file. Admittedly, it's not the stuff that keeps you awake at night, though I'm sure this trivia matters to somebody.

Other "firsts" are a bit more significant, capturing more of humanity's interest. Things that make the history books, such as

- First man on the moon (Neil Armstrong, 1969)
- First woman elected to the U.S. House of Representatives: Jeannette Rankin (1916, Montana)
- First black player in the major leagues: Jackie Robinson (1947)
- First man to reach the summit of Mt. Everest: Sir Edmund Hillary (1953)
- First athlete to run a mile in less than four minutes: Sir Roger Bannister (1954)
- First pilot to fly solo across the Atlantic: Charles Lindbergh (1927)

Of course, being first often means risk and sacrifice. It means being a trailblazer, a pioneer. Being first may mean suffering ridicule, isolation, loneliness, exposure, and even *death*.

Today, it's estimated that some 5,000 Christians are killed each year for their faith. The Old Testament lists many who died because of faith in Yahweh, but no one had yet been killed because of his faith in Christ.

Then came Stephen.

He was the first official Christian *martyr*, murdered by an angry mob because he stood for Jesus. For this reason, he occupies an honored place in Christian history.

WHEN "CAESAR" WAS MORE THAN A SALAD

To appreciate Stephen, we have to understand the times in which he lived. Christianity was still relatively new—so new that there was only one church! In fact, it wasn't even called "Christianity" yet. In those early years, it was called "the Way" (Acts 9:2; 19:9, 23; 22:4; 24:14, 22). Most early followers of Jesus were Jewish, and for them, living in the Roman Empire was kind of a "good news/bad news" thing. Good, because the mighty Roman Army protected you against foreign invasion. Rome had established relative peace in the world—building roads and making travel more accessible and commerce more prosperous. One language was spoken throughout the empire (Greek), making it easier to communicate with other countries. A bonus for Jews was that they were even allowed to practice their own religion.

The *bad* news was that the entire land was under the control of the Roman authorities. You were forced to obey all the Roman laws and pay high taxes. As long as you behaved, you were okay. But if Rome felt threatened, you might say "bye-bye" to your head.

Morally speaking, ancient Roman culture was just as decadent as ours. No, they didn't have pornography and sex on the Internet. But they had it everywhere else—in the marketplace, pagan temples, theatres, and arenas. You can see how it would've been a challenge for Christians to stay pure in a culture like that.

But there was another challenge for those early Christians. This challenge came not from Rome, but from the religious crowd. The majority of Christians came to Christ out of Judaism, but not all Jews became Christians. For most Jews, being Jewish was far more than just a religion. It also included their race, culture, and social customs. Everything about their identity was bound up in being Jewish, hanging with other Jews, and practicing Judaism. There wasn't a category in their minds for these new Christians who were born Jews who didn't conform to their Jewish sub culture. As a result, some Jewish religious leaders didn't tolerate anyone who abandoned the faith for this new "cult" that worshipped a dead teacher. In fact, they could get pretty violent about the subject.

FOOD FIGHT

It's in this religious scenario that the church experienced its first internal conflict. Here's what happened: The Jerusalem church was growing so fast that the apostles couldn't meet all the needs. Newly converted Jews who had come from Greece were mixed in the church with Jews from Jerusalem. The believers from Jerusalem thought they were *better* than those from Greece. As a result, poor widows from Greece were being ignored in the daily food distribution. They felt like victims of discrimination. Not happy campers.

So the apostles met and appointed seven men to oversee this matter. One of those men was Stephen, who was probably from Greece (not from Jerusalem). The apostles recognized something in him that made him worthy of consideration. Stephen is described in Acts 6:5 as a man "full of faith and of the Holy Spirit"; three verses later he's called "a man full of God's grace and power." In other words, he was the *total package*, an all-around great guy. So he and his six companions faithfully did their duty, serving and distributing the food to the needy. The apostles went back to their ministry. Problem solved. End of story, right? Not exactly.

Apparently, God had a ministry for Stephen beyond his duties as a church waiter. The Bible says he began doing "great wonders and miraculous signs among the people" (Acts 6:8). We're not sure exactly what these miracles were, but they probably included a lot of healings. Anyway, his activity really upset some unconverted Jews from Stephen's native country. They began arguing with him (something religious people love to do), but they couldn't stand up to the power and wisdom of his arguments. So they persuaded some men to tell lies about Stephen, hoping he would get arrested.

It worked.

Stephen was brought before the most powerful Jewish leaders in Jerusalem. The Sanhedrin was a council made up of 71 chief priests, elders, scribes, and lawyers.

It was like the Jewish version of our Supreme Court. Imagine being called before this intimidating group to testify! But instead of shivering in fear, Stephen stood with confidence, his face "like the face of an angel" (6:15).

He testified by giving them a thorough lesson in Jewish history. In fact, it's the longest sermon in the book of Acts! You can bet these scholars and leaders didn't like being schooled by this rookie religious instructor.

Toward the end of his message, Stephen really began pushing their buttons, saying things that made them furious. First, he claimed that God didn't live in a man-made house (Acts 7:48-49). In other words, there was no such thing as "God's house" any more. Instead, God lived in the heart and his temple was the body. (See 1 Corinthians 6:19.) Jews equated the worship of God with the temple, so Stephen's statement made them angry. Second, he told them they were a rebellious, proud people who didn't know God (Acts 7:51). Third, he accused them of murdering the prophets who foretold the Messiah's coming (7:52). He was not winning popularity points. Finally, he told them they were guilty of murdering the Son of God (7:52).

Okay, so they weren't going to elect Stephen class president or invite him to join them for a round of golf at the country club.

Quite the contrary. On hearing this, they were furious (literally "cut to the heart") and began gnashing their teeth at him! (7:54) Can you picture these men, so angry at Stephen that they're grinding their teeth? So furious that they are ready to drag him outside the city and stone him right then and there? Talk about anger management!

STAND IN THE PLACE WHERE YOU LIVE

You may have heard of people who, just before dying, describe seeing a bright light or scenes of heaven. Others describe a feeling of unusual peace. Of course, no one can prove these experiences are real. But it seems that Stephen must have had such an experience as he looked toward heaven and had a vision: "Look, I see heaven open and the Son of Man standing at the right hand of God" (Acts 7:56).

Stephen was about to die, and he knew it. The knowledge that one's life on this earth is about to be over is terrifying to some people. For Stephen, the realization that death was knocking at his door wasn't such a black thought. For him, the "grim reaper" wasn't so grim. Instead, his mind was filled with the sight of his Savior. But Jesus is portrayed differently here than he is elsewhere in Scripture. Though most post-resurrection portraits describe him as "seated at the right hand" of the Father (Ephesians 1:20), here Jesus is *standing,* a posture we see only two other times in the Bible (Revelation 5:6; 14:1).

But why?

I believe Jesus was standing to welcome Stephen home to heaven. Hey, there's nothing better than finally making it home after a long journey—and this beloved brother was about to pull into the driveway. And Jesus himself—*not* Saint Peter—was standing at the "pearly gates" to greet him.

I think there's a second reason Stephen sees Jesus standing. I think Jesus is standing in *honor* of Stephen. It's a standing ovation, as if Jesus is saying: *Stephen, you stood tall for me, so now I'll do the same for you. You confessed me before men on earth, so I'll confess you before heaven.* (See Matthew 10:32; Luke 12:8.) Jesus was demonstrating to all that Stephen was a man who deserved to be honored.

Stephen had stood firm against enormous peer pressure and personal opposition. It would've been easier to face a godless ruler or a Roman sword than persecution from your own people. But Stephen didn't flinch. He didn't shrink back or even blink. Instead, he looked his adversaries in the eyes and told the truth to men who had the power to kill him.

Stephen stood firm. In doing so, he lived the truth of Jesus' words: "All men will hate you because of me, but he who stands firm to the end will be saved" (Matthew 10:22).

Clearly, Steven had taken to heart the words of the apostle Paul, who later wrote

"Therefore, my dear brothers, stand firm. Let nothing move you. Always give yourselves fully to the work of the Lord, because you know that your labor in the Lord is not in vain" (1 Corinthians 15:58).

Why did Stephen have so much confidence to stand up for his faith? How did he do it? Well, Stephen had a *perspective* on life and a *passion* for God and his Word that few have today. He knew life was short, and only one thing really mattered: bringing honor to the name of Jesus Christ. For Stephen, Jesus wasn't just part of his life. Jesus *was* his life. Like Paul, Stephen's motto was "To live is Christ. To die is gain" (Gal. 2:20). Jesus was his *everything*, and nothing else came close. If he lost popularity because of his faith, so what? If he got in trouble because he shared truth, so what? If his stand for Christ cost him a relationship, so what?

Stephen knew Scripture and wasn't afraid to confront others with the truth. So what if they didn't agree? Stephen wasn't trying to please people, though he deeply cared about others. He wanted them to know Jesus as he did. And if taking a stand meant he had to suffer, so be it. Stephen had a one-track mind. Do you?

STICKS AND STONES...AND MORE STONES!

When Stephen mentioned his vision of Jesus at the right hand of God in heaven, the council exploded with rage. Covering their ears, they began screaming and rushing at him (Acts 7:57). In a moment of nearly unimaginable violence, that council became a self-appointed judge, jury, and executioner.

Dragging him outside the city, they began stoning him, a brutal execution style still practiced today in some countries. Each person involved

picked up any rock he or she could find and threw it as hard as possible at the guilty person. Since this person deserved to die, it didn't matter how cruel or brutal the hit. A blow to the head was especially celebrated, as the goal was to crush the skull. The community was encouraged to come and watch as a warning of the consequences of disobedience. The person being stoned suffered cuts, bruises, contusions, deep gashes, broken bones, massive loss of blood, and eventually loss of life. It is a horrific and painful way to die.

Imagine the adrenaline shooting through Stephen's body as hundreds of jagged rocks bombarded his body. There was no way to protect himself or deflect the blows. Showered by stones and feeling the hate with every painful hit, Stephen knew this was the end. So he prayed, "Lord Jesus, receive my spirit." He fell on his knees (apparently he had been standing the whole time!) and cried out, "Lord, do not hold this sin against them" (Acts 7:59-60).

Then he died.

Famous last words, echoing as testimony to what Christianity is all about. What an incredible way to go! He didn't shout, "Stop! I'm innocent!" or "God will judge you for this!" or "Somebody please help me!"

Who would've blamed him if he had?

Instead, between the excruciating thuds of those death rocks, Stephen managed one final sentence, words reminiscent of Christ's own statement from the cross, "Father, forgive them, for they do not know what they are doing" (Luke 23:34).

If Stephen's goal in life was to be like his Lord, he certainly made it. In a moment when most people would've freaked out and returned hatred with hatred, Stephen's heart was flooded with the trademark of the Christian faith—love.

His death became his ultimate gift of worship—and he became the first Christian to lose his life for Jesus. But Stephen's death marked more than his becoming the first martyr. Like a pack of wild animals, the angry religious crowd had acquired a taste for Christian blood. As a result, on that same day "a great persecution broke out against the church at Jerusalem, and all except the apostles were scattered throughout Judea and Samaria" (Acts 8:2).

If you recall, Jesus' last words to his disciples were to take the Good News about him to "all Judea and Samaria, and to the ends of the earth" (Acts 1:8). However, since the day Jesus returned to heaven, the disciples had remained in the relative safety of Jerusalem. It was their home turf, and they were happy to stay together and meet for church.

But they were disobedient.

So God used this tragic event and a dam of persecution came crashing down on the church. And this persecution scattered Christians where? *Throughout Judea and Samaria*. Hmm. Coincidence? I think not.

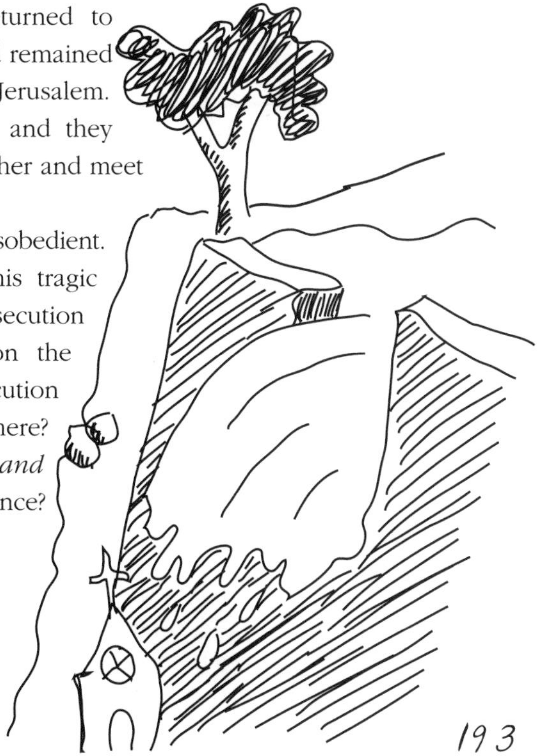

ANOTHER "STREAK"

More than a hundred years after Stephen's martyrdom, a well-educated man named Tertullian attended the gladiator games. That's where some men fought to the death while others were eaten alive by lions...all for the crowd's enjoyment. While watching uneducated men and little slave girls (all Christians) horribly killed this way, Tertullian began investigating Christianity and soon embraced the faith. Using his writing skills in defense of Christianity, he wrote these words: "The blood of the martyrs is the seed of the church."

It's a law of nature as strong and consistent as gravity itself: when one Christian gives his or her life for Jesus, the church is strengthened and more are brought to faith. Kill one Christian, and ten come to faith in Jesus.

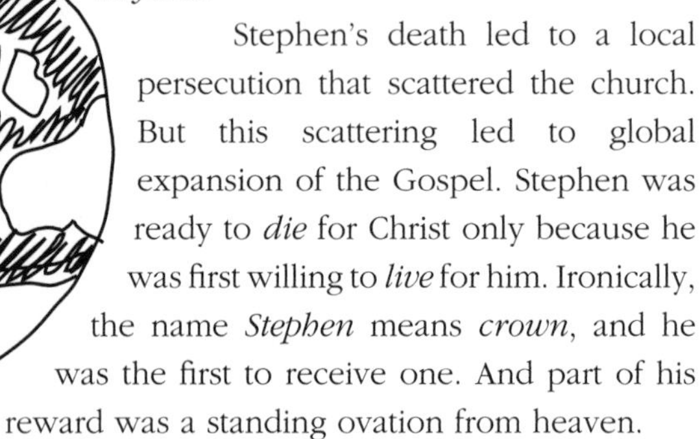

Stephen's death led to a local persecution that scattered the church. But this scattering led to global expansion of the Gospel. Stephen was ready to *die* for Christ only because he was first willing to *live* for him. Ironically, the name *Stephen* means *crown*, and he was the first to receive one. And part of his reward was a standing ovation from heaven.

I remember another standing ovation many years later. This one was on September 6, 1995. In many ways, it was just another baseball game at Camden Yards, Baltimore. The Orioles were playing the Angels. And Cal Ripken, Jr., was playing shortstop for the Orioles, just as he usually did. Nothing extraordinary about that.

But this was no ordinary game. With the previous night's game, Cal Ripken had tied the all-time major league record for consecutive games played—2,130 in a row, a record set by the legendary Lou Gehrig, and one that had stood for 56 years! So when the top of the fifth inning ended, and game 2,131 became official, Ripken's "streak" became one for the record books. Every one of the 46,272 fans in attendance that night rose to their feet in honor of the new "Iron Man."

For more than 22 minutes they cheered, clapping and crying in celebration. It was more than just a celebration of the moment. It was a tribute to the career of a legendary player.

Ripken emerged from the dugout several times, tipping his hat to the deafening applause. But it wasn't enough. The crowd wanted more, so Cal reluctantly stepped back onto the field to take a victory lap around the field, shaking hands and slapping "high fives" as he jogged. The Orioles later won 4-2, aided by a Ripken home run.

Friend, Jesus Christ sits on the edge of his throne in heaven, ready to welcome all those who faithfully serve him on earth. And I am confident he personally stands to greet every person who stood strong for him.

I believe there is a standing ovation in heaven waiting just for you.

Stephen had a perspective on life and a passion for God and his Word that few have today. For Stephen, Jesus wasn't just a part of his life. Jesus was his life. Jesus was his everything, and nothing else came close. So if he lost popularity because of his faith, so what? If he got in trouble because he shared truth, so what? If his stand for Christ cost him a relationship, so what?

Stephen had a one-track mind. Do you?

Ready to join?

We began this book with the story of a high school losing streak, and we ended with the story of a major league winner. So what kind of streak are you on? Maybe you've felt as if most of your life has been one big losing season. Or perhaps you're the kind of person who tends to enjoy success at nearly everything you do. That's okay, too. But eventually, all of us experience doubt, failure, and feelings of insignificance. We face them at school, home, work, on the team, and in our relationships. They are an unavoidable part of life.

So here's the real question: *What are you going to do when your faith weakens and you fumble in life's game?* I hope this book has helped you work through some answers to that question.

As we've traveled through the ups and downs of Scripture's strugglers, I hope you've made some new friends along the way—guys and girls who, through their own seasons of failure, discovered what it meant to "lose their lives" for a greater cause (Matthew 10:39). I trust that you now see them differently—not as perfect saints who never tasted failure or temptation, but as real people like you who worked through their doubts and discouragements to grow nearer to God. Funny, but it's to these people—along with the poor, the spiritually hungry, those who weep over sin and failure, and the persecuted—that Jesus promises the kingdom of God. All in all, we've learned a lot from Scripture's losers:

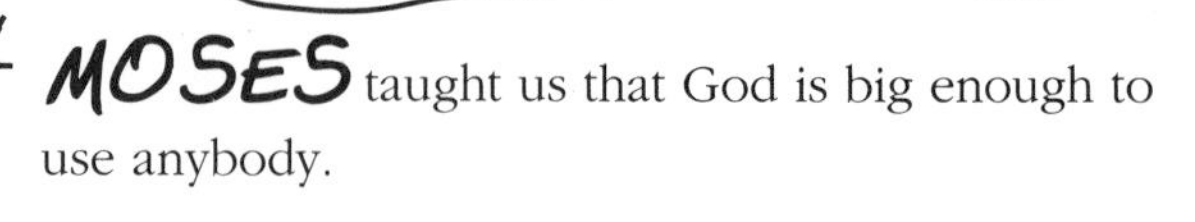

* **MOSES** taught us that God is big enough to use anybody.
* **DAVID** showed us how to be honest with God, even in our darkest days.
* **JOHN THE BAPTIST** let us know it's okay to doubt.
* **THOMAS** taught us the importance of Christian fellowship.
* **SOLOMON** showed us that only God can make us happy.
* **MARY MAGDALENE** proved we don't have to be weighed down by the past.
* **SAMSON** urged us to live up to our potential.

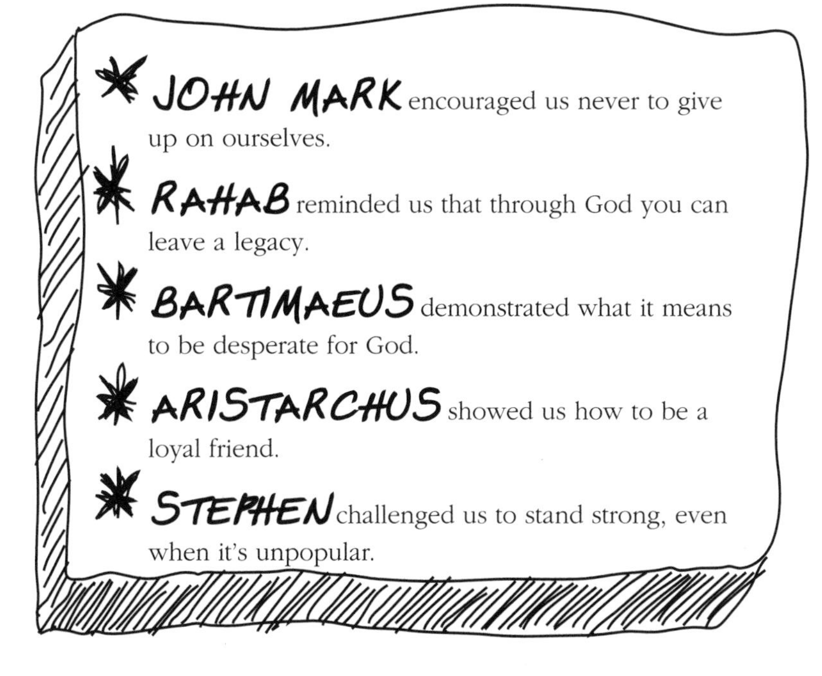

What these fragile men and woman have done is teach us *how to live*. I hope you realize now it's okay to be a loser, and that joining this club is the only true way to be a champion. These flesh-and-blood people have shown us that victories are often won in the valley.

We all struggle in this journey. But it's not the struggle, pain, and failure that define your identity. Rather, it's the *progress* toward Christ that makes you who you are.

Remember, you don't have to be a pro athlete to be great. You don't have to be famous, flashy, or fanatical. You don't even have to be first.

You just have to lose your life in him.

Will you?

We all struggle in this journey. But it's not the struggle, pain, and failure that define your identity. Rather, it's the progress toward Christ that makes you who you are.

IT'S NOT THAT YOU DON'T WANT TO READ THE BIBLE, MAYBE YOU JUST DON'T KNOW HOW.
ENJOY THE SILENCE
A 30 DAY EXPERIMENT IN LISTENING TO GOD
MAGGIE ROBBINS
DUFFY ROBBINS
.invert
ENJOY THE SILENCE'S 30 GUIDED EXERCISES PLUG YOU INTO THE ANCIENT DISCIPLINE OF LECTIO DIVINA. EACH LESSON PROVIDES A SELECTION OF SCRIPTURE, PROMPTS FOR MEDITATION, A CHANCE TO LISTEN TO GOD, AND A WAY TO RESPOND TO WHAT YOU'VE READ.
Enjoy the Silence
A 30 Day Experiment in Listening to God
Maggie Robbins, Duffy Robbins
RETAIL $9.99
ISBN 0-310-25991-6
.invert
Visit www.invertbooks.com or your local bookstore.